A PEEP INTO THE EARLY HISTORY OF INDIA

A PEEP INTO THE EARLY HISTORY OF INDIA

From the Foundation of the Maurya Dynasty to the Downfall of the Imperial Gupta Dynasty.

(322 B. C. — circa 500 A. C.)

By

SIR R. G. BHANDARKAR,

M.A., Ph. D., K.C.I.E.

WITH A PREFACE

BY

H. G. RAWLINSON,

Principal, Karnatak College, DHARWAR.

GYAN

Published by

GYAN

Gyan Publishing House
5, Ansari Road
Daryaganj, New Delhi-110002
Phone: 011-47034999, 9811692060
E-mail: books@gyanbooks.com

Distribution Network
gyanbooks.com
India, USA, Canada, UK, Australia, France

ISBN : 978-81-212-2580-9 (HB)
First Published, 1920

2nd Impression 2021

Printed at: Gyan Press, Delhi.

A Peep into the Early History of India
Author: Sir R. G. Bhandarkar

A PEEP INTO THE EARLY HISTORY OF INDIA

From the Foundation of the Maurya Dynasty to the Downfall of the Imperial Gupta Dynasty.

(322 B.C.—*circa* 500 A.C.)

BY

SIR R. G. BHANDARKAR, M.A., Ph. D., K.C.I.E., &c.

WITH A PREFACE

BY

H. G. RAWLINSON,

Principal, Karnatak College, DHARWAR.

BOMBAY

D. B. TARAPOREVALA SONS, AND Co.

1920.

PREFACE.

Sir Ramkrishna Bhandarkar's *Peep into the Early History of India*, like his monumental contribution to the Bombay Gazetteer on the Early History of the Deccan, has become a classic of its kind. Delivered originally in Poona in the form of a lecture nineteen years ago, it subsequently appeared in the pages of the Journal of the Bombay Branch of the Royal Asiatic Society. It is a model of lucid writing upon what might otherwise easily become a wearisome and complicated subject, and for this reason it forms an admirable introduction to the study of the period. A student who starts with this bird's-eye view may proceed with less diffidence to the more detailed accounts in works such as Mr. V. A. Smith's, and to original authorities like McCrindle's Megasthenes. One of Sir Ramkrishna's objects is to call the attention of his countrymen to the necessity of using the information supplied by coins, inscriptions and archæological remains, and the writings of foreign travellers, in reconstructing the past history of their land. As is well-known, the science of history finds no place in orthodox Sanskrit learning, and it was not until western scholars drew attention to these matters that any steps were taken in this direction. But with the spread of modern ideas, it remains for Indian Students to take upon their own shoulders these branches of research. To such, Sir Ramkrishna's advice is invaluable at the present day, when the revived spirit of Indian nationalism inclines writers to fasten eagerly upon any facts which tend to the glory of their past civilization. Nothing is more fatal to the historian than the patriotic bias, for it invariably leads him to form prejudiced and unjustified conclusions. "Nothing but dry truth should be his object", says this distinguished scholar, who has so resolutely practised in his writings what he here preaches, and it is to be hoped that the younger generation which is following in his steps will be not unmindful of his words.

The essay begins with the rise of Buddhism. As Sir Ramkrishna points out, Buddhism is only a sect of Hinduism. Its tenets are not even novel. Its chief doctrine, *viz.* that it is *karma* which transmigrates, is anticipated in the Upanishads. It did not, contrary to popular opinion, seek to undermine caste. But it *did* deny the authority of the Vedas and the efficacy of the Vedic sacrifices, and this was the real cause of the hatred of the Brahmans towards it. Buddhism, with its insistence on the ethical side of religion and its cosmopolitanism, had a salutary effect on Indian politics. It encouraged liberal intercourse with the outside world which Brahmanism discouraged. Under the various Buddhistic dynasties, shipping flourished, ambassadors went and came to and from Syria and Egypt, and later, Rome. The Bodhisatva himself, according to the *Jâtakas*, was once born as the son of a master-mariner of Broach. The Bodhisatva and Jains, like the Puritans of 17th century England, were the trading-classes. Sir Ramkrishna mentions in his essay on the Early History of the Deccan how much the great cathedral caves of Karla and other places in Western India owed to the guilds of merchants of the time. With the Brahmanic revival and the insertion in the codes of Manu of regulations which branded those who ventured overseas with the stigma of impurity, commerce declined and India dropped out of her position among the trading nations of the East.

The greatness of India commences with the Maurya dynasty. Of Chandragupta, the author does not say very much. But his reign is of great importance, if only on account of the marked influence that Persian culture exerted upon India at that time. Chandragupta's vast and complicated bureaucracy was organized upon most efficient lines, but those who look upon India's past as Golden Age, would do well to consider the oppressive tyranny and the cruel severity of the whole system. Sir Ramkrishna was, of course, writing long before the epoch-making discovery of the *Artha Śâstra* (whether this be a genuine product of the pen of Kautilya or not) threw a flood of new light on the problem of Mauryan administration. On Asoka, on the other hand, the author is very clear and explicit, and his summary is most interesting. With the break-up of the Mauryan Empire, a number of tribes from Central Asia, the Yavanas or Bactrian Greeks, the Sakas, the Kshatrapas, the Parthians and the Kushans found their way through the North-West frontier into the Panjab and Western India. With the Kushans, the long supremacy of Buddhism came gradually to an end. The simple teaching of the Hinayana system had been replaced by the vast and complicated pantheon of the Mahayana, and the time was ripe for a Brahmanic revival. This came under the Guptas, and the author fitly concludes his essay with an account of the great literary Renaissance of that period.

Archæology is an ever-growing science, and, as we have indicated above, there are many points in which subsequent discoveries have modified or thrown open to doubt some of the statements made when this essay was published nineteen years ago. On one only, however, is there likely to be any serious difference of opinion. Mr. V. A. Smith in his *Early History of India* supports the theory that Kanishka's accession took place in A. D. 78, *i. e.* that the Saka era dates from his coming to the throne. It is now, however, generally held that the first Kushan Monarch was Kadphises I, *c.* A. D. 40-78, and the second was Kadphises II, A. D. 78-110. Thus the Saka Era was founded not by Kanishka but by Kadphises II. Kanishka succeeded about A. D. 120 and reigned till about 182. The Kushan Empire broke up at the death of Vasudeva, about 220. Sir Ramkrishna has always stood out for a later date for the Kushans. He thinks that the Saka Era was founded by a Saka King: that the Saka and Indo-Parthian dynasties intervened, and the Kushans belong to the third and fourth centuries A. C. However, *adhuc sub judice lis est,* and we must await the further revelations of archæology for a final answer.

H. G. RAWLINSON.

Dharwar, 1919.

INTRODUCTORY.[1]

I think I may take it for granted that an Indian who has received English education and has been introduced to the ancient history of European countries, naturally has a desire to be acquainted with the ancient history of his own country, to know by whom and how that country was governed in ancient times, or how its social and religious institutions have grown up and what revolutions the country has gone through; but means for the satisfaction of this desire are wanting. India unfortunately has no written history. There are some chronicles written by Jainas and others referring to kings and princes who lived from about the eighth to the eleventh centuries of the Christian era and ruled over Gujarat and Rajputana. There are also lives of individual kings such as the Śrî-Harshacharita of Bâna and the Vikramâṅkadevacharita of Bilhaṇa. The hero of the former ruled over Northern India in the first half of the seventh century, and of the latter over Southern India in the latter part of the eleventh and the early part of the twelfth century. The Purânas contain genealogies of certain dynasties. With these exceptions, sometime ago we had absolutely no knowledge of the history of the different provinces of India before the foundation of the Mahomedan Empire. But the researches of European and some Native scholars and antiquarians have thrown considerable light over this dark period. The knowledge hitherto gathered cannot be pronounced to be very satisfactory or to be as good as written books would have supplied. Still, it is sufficient to give us a general idea of the political, social,

1 This article consists of a lecture read in March last (1910) before a Poona audience, but afterwards considerably amplified.

and religious movements that took place from remote times to the arrival of the Mahomedans. The materials for these researches I shall here shortly describe.

First,—Gold, silver and copper coins of ancient kings are found in all parts of the country, especially in Northern India, when old mounds composed of the ruins of buildings are dug out. These coins bear certain emblems, and also legends in ancient characters containing the names of the Princes who issued them, and sometimes of their fathers, with occasionally the date of their issue. From these we derive a knowledge of the kings and dynasties that ruled over the provinces in which the coins are found.

Secondly,—We find inscriptions engraved on rocks and columns and on the remains of ancient temples wherein occur the names of Princes, and sometimes of the provinces ruled over or conquered by them. In the case of temples and other benefactions we have the names of the donors, their profession, the description of the nature of their gift and sometimes the name of the king in whose reign the gift was made. Again, we find in digging old ruins, charters of land-grants made by Princes, inscribed on plates of copper. The grants therein recorded were made to individual Brahmans or to temples or Buddhistic Vihâras. These copper-plate inscriptions often give a full genealogy of the dynasty to which the grantor belonged, together with the most notable events in the reign of each of the princes belonging to the dynasty. Often-times, there is a mere vague praise of the different kings which can have no historical value but one who possesses a little critical power can without much difficulty distinguish between what is historically true and what is not. A very large number of such grants has been found in our own Maratha country, in consequence of which we have been able to construct a sort of continuous political history from about the beginning of the sixth century to the time of the Mahomedan invasion.

Thirdly,—Another important source consists the writings of foreigners who visited this country or obtained information about it from others. The invasion of Alexander the Great brought the Greeks into communication with India, and after his death his general Seleucus who obtained the province of Syria kept up a regular intercourse with a king who is called Sandracottus by the Greeks, who reigned at Pâṭaliputra, and at whose court resided an ambassador of Seleucus of the name of Megasthenes. The work of Megasthenes, though not extant, was abridged by other writers and in this form it has come down to us. Then we have Ptolemy's Geography which was written between 151 and 163 A. C., the date of his death. He gives names of Indian towns and sometimes of the princes who reigned there at the time. Similarly we have got another work called the Periplus of the Erythrean Sea, whose author is unknown. He too gives valuable geographical and historical information After Buddhism had penetrated into China, several Chinese pilgrims visited India from time to time and have left us an account of what they saw. Such are Fa Hian, Sung-yun, Hiuen Tsiang, and Itsing. The Mahomedans who visited the country in later times have also left us similar works. Besides the information given by these writers about the people, their literature, and their kings, what is of the highest value is the help they afford in determining the dates of events in India. For all these foreigners had good systems of chronology.

Besides these, some of the later Sanskrit and vernacular works contain what are called Prasâstis or historical accounts of princes in whose reign they were composed and sometimes of the dynasties to which they belonged

These are the authorities for the political history of the country; but the history of thought as well as of religious and social institutions is to be gathered from the literature itself, which is vast. But though it is vast, still older works calculated to enable us to solve many problems in literary and social history have perished.

In using all these materials, however, one should exercise a good deal of keen critical power. No one who does not possess this power can make a proper use of them. A good many years ago, I delivered a lecture on the critical and comparative method of study, which has been published. To what I have stated there, I shall only add that in dealing with all these materials one should proceed on such principles of evidence as are followed by a judge. One must in the first place be impartial, with no particular disposition to find in the materials before him something that will tend to the glory of his race and country, nor should he have an opposite prejudice against the country or its people. Nothing but dry truth should be his object; and he should in every case determine the credibility of the witness before him and the probability or otherwise of what is stated by him. He should ascertain whether he was an eye-witness or a contemporary witness, and whether in describing a certain event he himself was not open to the temptation of exaggeration or to the influence of the marvellous. None of the current legends should be considered to be historically true, but an endeavour should be made to find any germ of truth that there may be in them by evidence of another nature.

THE MAURYAS.

I shall now proceed to give a short sketch of the history of India as determined by the critical use of these materials. As I have already observed, the Puranas give lists of kings who, they say in prophetic language, will reign in the future. In consequence of the corruption of manuscripts there are a great many discrepancies in the lists as given in different works of that class. Besides, there is no chronological clue whatever to be found in them. We will, therefore, begin with that dynasty of which we have intimation elsewhere, and with that king whose date can be determined by unimpeachable evidence Chandragupta is mentioned as the founder of the Maurya dynasty. He is said to have uprooted the family of the Nandas who ruled before him and to have been assisted by a Brahman of the name of Chânakya. He is one of those whose memory has been preserved by both Buddhist and Brahmanic writers. We have a dramatic play in which his acquisition of the throne through the help of Chânakya is alluded to. Buddhistic works also give similar accounts about him. The grammarian Patanjali alludes to the Mauryas and speaks of a *Chandraguptasabhâ.* In an inscription, dated in the year 72, which has been referred to the Śaka era and is consequently equivalent to 150 A. D., Chandragupta the Maurya is spoken of as having caused a certain tank to be constructed; and we have contemporary evidence also of the existence of the king and of his acquisition of the throne in the writings of Greek authors. They speak of Chandragupta as being an ambitious man in his youth, and as having been present in the Panjab at the time of Alexander's invasion. He is said to have freed the country from the Macedonian yoke, to have fought with Seleucus, who had obtained the Syrian province of the Alexandrian empire, and to have finally concluded a treaty with him. Seleucus sent an ambassador to his court of the name of Megasthenes. From this connection of Chandragupta with Seleucus we have been able to determine the date of his accession, which is about 322

B. C. Chandragupta's capital was Pâṭaliputra, which is represented by Greek writers to have been situated at the confluence of the Ganges and the Erannoboas, which last corresponds to our Hiranyabâhâ. Hiranyabâhâ was another name of the Sona, and Patañjali speaks of Pâṭaliputra as situated on the banks of the Soṇa.[2] His successor, according to one Purâṇa, was Bindusâra, and, according to another, Bhadrasâra. He is mentioned also in Buddhistic works, but the name does not occur in any inscription or foreign writing. His son was called Aśoka. This is a very important name in the ancient history of the whole of India, and as the connection of the prince with Buddhism was close, and that religion plays an important part in the general history of India, I must here give a short account of it.

RISE OF BUDDHISM—ITS DOCTRINES AND AIMS.

After the Indian Âryas had established the system of sacrificial religion fully, their speculation took its start from the sacrifice. Every thing was identified with some sacrificial operation. The gods are represented in the Purusha Sûkta to have sacrificed the primordial Purusha, from whom thus sacrificed arose the whole creation. *Brahman* is a word which in the Ṛiksaṁhitâ means a particular Mantra or verse addressed to a god, or that sort of power from which one is able to compose such a Mantra. Thence it came to signify the true power or virtue in a sacrifice, or its essence; and when the whole universe was regarded as produced from a kind of sacrifice, its essence also came to be named *Brahman*. There was at the same time religious and philosophical speculation upon an independent basis starting from the self-conscious soul. In the Ṛigveda Saṁhitâ we have several philosophical hymns, and the speculation which they

2 अनुशोणं पाटलिपुत्रम्.

indicate ran on in its course, and the results of it we have in the Upanishads. In the celebrated hymn beginning with *Nâsadâsînnosadâsît*[3] it is represented that in the darkness which enveloped the whole worlds in the beginning, that which was wrapped up in the Unsubstantial developed through the force of brooding energy, and there arose in it a Desire which is spoken of as the first germ of the mind. This idea that our worldly existence with its definite modes of thinking is the result of desire developed in a variety of ways. This appears to be the idea adopted or appropriated by Buddhism, and one sense of the name Mâra of the Buddhistic Prince of Darkness is Kâma or desire. Of the four noble truths of Buddhism the first is misery (Duhkha), and the second the origin of misery. This is thirst or desire. If, therefore, the misery of worldly existence is due to desire, the conclusion follows that, in the words of the Kathâ Upanishad, by uprooting your desire you are free from misery and attain immortality and eternal bliss. This is the third of the noble truths. But immortality or eternal bliss one can speak of when one regards the soul as something different from and lying beyond the mind or thoughts which have been set in motion by desire. When, however, the existence of such a thing beyond the mind or thought is denied, the condition of eternal bliss means, when thought has ceased, what some people call annihilation. In one of the sections of the Brihadâranyaka, which Upanishad and the Chhândogya might be regarded as collections of the speculations of various Ṛishis, there occurs a passage which comes very near to the denial of the soul as a separate substance. "Yâjñavalkya," says Ârtabhâga, the son of Jaratkâru, "when the speech of a man or Puru-

3 Rv. X 129

यदा सर्वे प्रमुच्यन्ते कामा येऽस्य हृदि स्थिता &c. Katha U. VI., 14.

sha who is dead, goes to Agni or fire, his breath to the wind, his sight to the sun, his mind to the moon, his power of hearing to the quarters, the body to the earth, and the self to the Akâsa or ether, the hairs of his body to the herbs and the hairs on the head to the trees, and the blood and seminal fluid are placed in the waters, where does the Purusha exist?" Yâjñavalkya answers "Ârtabhâga, give me your hand. We alone shall know of this and not the people here." So then they went out and conversed with each other and what they spoke of was Karma (deeds), and what they praised was Karma. He who does meritorious Karma or deeds becomes holy, and he who does sinful deeds becomes sinful. With this Ârtabhâga, the son of Jaratkâru, was satisfied and remained silent.[5] Here it will be seen that the different parts of which man is composed are represented as being dissolved into the different parts of the Cosmos, and what remains is the Karma. The ideas therefore involved in this dialogue are three:—(1) That the soul is not a substance separate from the component parts of a human being; (2) that what renders transmigration or the production of a new being possible is the Karma, and (3) that according to the nature of the previous Karma is the nature of the new being, holy or sinful. The third idea is common to all Hindu systems of philosophy or religion; but the first two are heterodox, and must have been considered so when the dialogue was composed, since it was to avoid the shock which the exposition of such doctrines would cause that Yâjñavalkya retires from the assembly and speaks to Ârtabhâga alone. Still the ideas had been developed in the times of the Upanishad and were adopted by Buddhism. In the celebrated dialogue between the Greek king Milinda or Menander of Sâkala and Nâgasena, a Buddhist Saint, the king asks: "How is your

5 Br. Ar. Up. III, 2, 13-14.

reverence known? What is your name?" Nāgasena replies: "I am called Nâgasena by my parents, the priests, and others. But Nâgasena is not a separate entity." And going on further in this way Nâgasena gives an instance of the chariot in which the king came, and says: "As the various parts of a chariot when united form the chariot, so the five Skandhas, when united in one body form a being or living existence." Here we see that as there is nothing like a chariot independently of its parts, so there is nothing like a man independently of the various elements of which he is composed. Further on in the same book we have, "The king said, 'what is it, Nâgasena, that is re-born?' 'Name-and-form is re-born 'What, is it this same name-and-form that is re-born?' 'No; but by this name-and-form deeds are done, good and evil, and by these deeds (this Karma) another name-and-form is re-born.[7]" In the external world also the Buddhist believes in the existence of no substance. To him all knowledge is phenomenal, and this is what appears to be meant by the doctrine that every thing is *Kshanika* or momentary.

But it was not the metaphysical doctrines of Buddhism that influenced the masses of the people. What proved attractive was its ethical side. The Buddhist preachers discoursed on *Dharma* or righteousness to the people. Such discourses on *Dharma* without the introduction of any theistic idea have their representatives in the Brahmanic literature. In many of the episodes of the Mahâbharata, especially in the Sânti and Anusas anika books,

6. The five Skandhas are रूप physical constituents, विज्ञान self-consciousness. वेदना feeling of pleasure or pain, संज्ञा name, and संस्कार love, hatred, and infatuation. These five constitute the human being.

7. नामरूप or name-and-form is equivalent to the five Skandhas of which a living being is composed. The expression, therefore, signifies a living individual.

we have simply ethical discourses without any reference to God, of the nature of those we find in Buddhistic works; and sometimes the verses in the Mahâbhârata, are the same as those occurring in the latter. There appears to be at one time a period in which the thoughts of the Hindus were directed to the delineation of right conduct in itself without any theistic bearing. And Buddhism on its ethical side represents that phase. Right conduct is the last of the four noble truths of Buddhism. The origin of misery alluded to above is destroyed by what is called the eight-fold Path—*viz.*, right views, right resolve, right speech, right action, right living, right effort, right self-knowledge, right contemplation.[8] Thus the Buddhistic gospel is, that righteous conduct is the means of the destruction of suffering which may end in positive happiness or not according as one regards his soul as substantial or phenomenal. It was this phase of Buddhism that with the strenuous efforts of the missionaries and of the Emperor Asoka enabled it to achieve success amongst the masses of the people; and what was wanting on the theistic side was supplied by the perfection and marvellous powers attributed to the founder of the religion. Without this faith in the perfection or, what we should call, the divine nature of Buddha, a mere ethical religion would probably not have succeeded. Buddhism was not a social revolution as has been thought by some writers. It was a religion established and propagated by persons who

8 सम्यग्दृष्टिः, सम्यक्संकल्पः, सम्यग्वाक्, सम्यक्कर्मान्तः सम्यगाजीवः, साम्यग्वायामः सम्यक्स्मृतिः, सम्यक्समाधिश्च । The true sense of सम्यक्स्मृतिः has, it appears to me, not yet been correctly given, स्मृति is remembrance of what a man's true condition is; being blinded to it is स्मृतिविभ्रम or स्मृतिभ्रंशः Bhag. G. ii. 63. Seeing where one's course of conduct is leading one and remembering what one ought to do is स्मृति; and that is awakened in one by God; *Ib.* xv. 15. When infatuation disappears, स्मृति returns. *Ib.* xviii. 73.

had renounced the world and professed not to care for it. From times of old there existed in the Indian community such persons, who were called Śramanas and belonged originally to all castes. These gave themselves to contemplation and sometimes propounded doctrines of salvation not in harmony with the prevalent creed. Buddhism was not even a revolt against caste, for though men from all castes were admitted to the monastic order, and though in the discourses of Buddha himself and others the distinction of caste is pronounced to be entirely worthless, still the object of those who elaborated the system was not to level caste-distinctions. They even left the domestic ceremonies of their followers to be performed according to the Vedic ritual. This is one of the arguments brought against Buddhism by Udayanâchârya. "There does not exist," he says, "a sect, the followers of which do not perform the Vedic rites beginning with the Garbhâdhana and ending with the funeral, even though they regard them as having but a relative or tentative truth." Buddhism, however, was a revolt against the sacrificial system and denied the authority of the Vedas as calculated to point out the path to salvation. And this is at the root of the hostility between itself and Brahmanism.

PROPAGATION OF BUDDHISM,—ASOKA'S EDICTS.

Buddhism was propagated by a number of devoted persons. But I think the efforts of Aśoka contributed a good deal to its acceptance by the large mass of the people. Though of course in his edicts he does not inculcate upon his people faith in Buddha and Samgha

9 नास्त्येव तद्दर्शनं यत्र सांवृतमतेदित्युक्त्वापि गर्भाधानाद्यन्त्येष्टिपर्यन्तां वैदिकीं क्रियां जनो नानुतिष्ठति । Atmatattvaviveka, Calc. Ed. of Samvat 1956, p. 89, सांवृत relating to ति, a Buddhist technical term,

still the Dharma or righteousness that he preaches is in the spirit of Buddhism. The inscriptions of Aśoka are engraved on rocks, pillars, and tablets of stone. Those of the first class are found at Girnâr in Kāthiâwâḍ on the west, Shahbazgarhi and Mansehra on the North-West frontiers of the Panjab, Khalsi near the sources of the Jumna in the Himalaya, Dhauli in Katak, and Jaugaḍ in Ganjam on the east. All these contain the same edicts, their number in some cases being fourteen, and less in others. In the last two places there are two separate edicts not found on the other rocks. These inscriptions are in two different characters—those at Girnar, Khalsi, Dhauli and Jaugad being in the character called Brahmî, which is the earliest form of our modern Devanagari, and those at Shahbazgarni and Mansehra are in the character called Kharoshṭhi, and are written from right to left in the manner of the ancient Pahlavi and the modern Persian and Arabic documents. Two of the columns bearing inscriptions of the second class are now at Dehli. They were brought there by the Emperor Firozshah from Siwalik and Merat. The others exist at Allahabad, Radhia, Mathia, and Râmpurva. The edicts are the same on these columns, but the number of these on the Siwalik Delhi pillar is seven, the second Dehli pillar contains five, that at Râmpurvâ four, and the rest six. In the case of both these classes, the inscriptions are well-preserved in some cases and mutilated in others. Smaller edicts on rocks are found at Rûpnâth and Sahasaram in Bhagelkhand, Bairat on the north-eastern boundary of Rajputana, Siddapur in the Maisur territory and Maski in the Nizam's Dominions. There is also a tablet inscription addressed to the Mâgadha Samgha, and three small ones in caves at Barabar near Gaya. Two more inscriptions have been found at Paderia and Niglîva in the Nepâl Terai.

EXTENT OF ASOKA'S EMPIRE AND THE DATE OF HIS CORONATION.

Now, in the first place, from the localities in which we find these inscriptions it appears that Aśoka's dominions extended from Kâthiâwaḍ on the west to Katak and Ganjam on the east, and to Afghanistan, Panjab, and the sources of the Jumna in the north. To the south it extended over the centre of the table-land of the Dekkan up to Maisur. In the second rock-edict he speaks of "*conquered*" countries and the "neighbouring or bordering" countries. In the last class he mentions the Chodas, the Pandyas, Satiyaputa, Ketalaputa or Keralaputa up to Tambapaṇṇi, and the countries of Antiyoko the Yona king and his neighbours. In the thirteenth rock-edict he speaks of his having achieved religious victory "here" and in the neighbouring or bordering countries up to six hundred *Yojanas*, where reigns Antiyoko, the Yona king, and further away from him where the four kings, Turamâya, Antikina, Maka and Alikasudara hold sway, and down below where the Choda and the Pândya rule up to Tambapaṇṇi, and also in the countries of "Hidarâja." This last expression must be translated by "the kings about here," among whom he enumerates those of the countries of Visha, Vaji, Yona, Kamboja, Nâbhâta, Nabhapanti, Bhoja Pitinika, Andhra, and Pulinda.[10] Here there is a three-fold division, *viz.*, his own empire,

10 Epigr. Ind. Vol. II. pp. 449-450 and 462-465. Hidarâja has been taken to be a proper name by both M. Senart and Dr. Bühler. But *Hida* everywhere in these inscriptions means "here," and the sense the "kings here "fits in very well with the context. As'oka distinguishes between *Hida* and *Antesu—i. e.*, his own empire and the territories of his neighbours The third class left must be of those who were kings in the extent of country that could be spoken of as *Hida*, *i. e.*, princes comprised in his empire or dependent princes. Ib. p. 471, and Inscriptions of Piyadasi, by Senart, Vol. II. p. 84, and p. 92, note 63,

spoken of as "here"; the neighbouring independent countries ruled over by Antiochus and others, and those of the Chodas and Pândyas; and the "Hidarâjas" or "kings here," *i. e.*, in his empire. On comparing both these passages, it would appear that Antiochus and the other Greek princes as well as the princes of the Chodas and Pândyas, were independent; while the kings of the Vajjis, whose country lay near Pâṭaliputra, and of the Bhojas, the Petenikas, and the Andhras and the Pulindas were under his influence, *i. e.*, were probably his feudatories; while the rest of the country was under his immediate sway. Among the feudatory princes must also be included those of the Gandhâras, Râsṭikas, and the Aparantas, who are mentioned in the fifth rock-edict, and to whose dominions he sent overseers of righteousness.[11] From the mention of Antiyoko and others in the second and thirteenth edicts, the date when they were composed can be accurately determined. Antiyoko was Antiochus of Syria (260—247 B. C.), Turamâya was Ptolemy Philadelphus of Egypt (285—247 B. C.) Antikini was Antigonus Gonatus of Macedonia (278—242 B. C.), Maka was Magas of Cyrene (died 258 B. C.), and Alikasudara was Alexander of Epirus (died between 262 and 258. All of those were living between 260 and 258) B. C., wherefore the matter in the inscription was composed between those years, *i. e.*, about 259 B. C., and Aśoka was crowned about 271 B. C., as the edict was promulgated in the thirteenth year after the event.[12]

AŚOKA, A BUDDHIST, BUT TOLERANT AND LIBERAL.

In the edicts at Sahasarâm, Bairat, Rûpnâth and Siddapur,[13] Aśoka says that he was an *Upâsaka* or lay-

11 धर्ममहामात्राः

12 Inscriptions of Pyadasi, by Senart, Vol. II. p. 86, Eng. Trans.

13 Ind. Ant. Vol. XXII. pp. 302-303; Inscr. of P. Vol. II. pp. 57-58 and 67; and Ep. Ind. Vol. IV. III. p. 138,

follower of Buddhism for more than two years and a half, but did not exert himself to promote righteousness; but for more than a year afterwards he did so, and the result was that those men and gods that had been regarded as true in Jambudvîpa before, were rendered false. In the eighth rock-edict, he speaks of his having "set out for Sambodhi," which technically means perfect knowledge, after the end of the tenth year since his coronation. This expression occurs in Buddhistic Pali works, and signifies "beginning to do such deeds as are calculated to lead in the end to perfection." From these two statements it appears that Aśoka was a Buddhistic lay follower; and worked with a view to gain the highest good promised by Buddhism. He visited the Lumbinî grove, where Sâkyamuni was born, after he had been a crowned king for twenty years, and, having done worship, erected a stone column on the site with a stone enclosure (enclosing wall)[14] Paderia, in the Nepâl Terai, where the inscription which mentions this was found engraved on a mutilated pillar, must be the site of the birth-place of Buddha. The other Nepâl inscription that was found at Niglîva represents his having increased the stûpa raised to Konâkamana, when fourteen years had elapsed since his coronation, and some years afterwards, probably in the same year in which he visited the Lumbinî grove, he did worship there.[15] In the Bâbhra inscription addressed to the Magâdha Church, Aśoka expresses his faith in the Buddhist Triad of Buddha, Dharma (Righteousness), and Saṃgha (the Assembly), and recommends that certain works which he names should be read and pondered over

14 Ep. Ind. Vol. V. p. 4. I think. सिलाविगडभीचा must be an enclosure or railing made of stone. भीचा is probably connected with भित्ति or भित्तिक "a wall."

15 Ep. Ind. Vol. V. pp. 5-6.

16 Ind. Ant. Vol. V. p. 257.

by the priests as well as by lay followers.[16] All this shows distinctly enough that Aśoka was a Buddhist; but in the edicts his nations seem to be so liberal and exalted, and his admission that there is truth in the teachings of all sects is so plain, that it must be concluded that he was not actuated by a sectarian spirit, but by a simple respect for truth; and his ethical discourses were such as to be acceptable to everybody, and his moral overseers worked amongst people of all classes and creeds.

AŚOKA'S AIMS AND OBJECTS AND THE MEANS HE EMPLOYED.

Asoka's great object in publishing his edicts was to preach and promote righteousness amongst his subjects. Dharma or righteousness consists, as said by him, in the second pillar-edict, (1) in doing no ill, (2) doing a great deal of good, (3) in sympathy, (4) beneficence, (5) truth, and (6) purity. In the seventh edict he adds, (7) gentleness, and (8) saintliness[17] Besides this, he prohibited the killing of animals for religious sacrifices, and was very particular about it.[18] In the fifth pillar-edict he does seem to allow the flesh of certain animals to be used, but he carefully enumerates those that should not be killed at all, and the conditions under which others should not be killed at all, and the conditions under which others should not be killed. Large feasts or banquets, where hundreds of thousands of animals were killed, he prohibited.[19] He directed his officers to go on tours every

17 Ep. Ind. Vol. II. pp. 249, 269-71, and also Inscr. Piy. Vol. II. pp. 6, 26-27. The words are : (1) अपासीनव, (2) बहुकयेाण (बहुकल्याण), (3) दया,(4) दान, (5) सच (सत्य), (6) सोचये (शौच), (7) मदबे (मार्दव), and (8) साधवे (साधुत्व).

18 1st Rock Edict and also the 4th.

19 1st Rock Edict.

five years for the inculcation of Dharma or righteousness and for other matters. He had Mahâmâtras or Governors of provinces before, but in the fifth rock-edict he speaks of his having created the office of Dharmamahâmâtras of overseers of righteousness in the fourteenth year after his coronation, and sent them to different countries—those under his immediate sway and those which were semi-independent. They were to work amongst old and young, rich and poor, householders and recluses, and amongst the followers of the different sects; an their business was to look to the good of all, to establish and promote righteousness, and to protect all from oppression. They were also to work amongst those who were near to him, in his family, and amongst his relations. In the fourth rock-edict he tells us that by his efforts the destruction of animals, which was enormous before, has almost ceased by his religious orders or instructions, and a regard for one's relations for Brahmans and Sramanas or holy recluses, obedience to father and mother and to the old, and general righteousness have increased and will increase, and he hopes that his sons, grandsons, and great-grandsons, &c., up to the end of the Kalpa will go on promoting it; and, being righteous themselves, will instruct their subjects in righteousness. For, "this," he says, "is the highest duty one can perform, *viz.*, that of preaching righteousness." In the seventh rock-edict he allows the followers of all sects to live wherever they like, because what they all aim at is self-restraint and purity; and in the twelfth he says that he shows his regard for the members of all sects, for the recluses and householders, by gifts and in various other ways; but the highest or the best way of showing regard is to seek to increase the importance of all sects. This importance is increased by ceasing to extol one's own sect or revile that of another, and by showing respect for the creed of another. Aśoka also speaks of his having planted trees and medicinal herbs, dug wells, and opened establishments for the distribution of water, for the good of men and animals in different places, even in the countries of his foreign neighbours.[20] The inscriptions in two of the caves at Barâbar mention their being dedicated after he had been a crowned monarch for twelve years to the use of members of the Ajîvakdi sect, which like that of the Buddhists, was a sect of recluses; that in the third does not give any name.[21]

This will give the reader an idea of the sort of religion preached by Aśoka. He prohibited animal sacrifices and aught that right conduct was the only way to heaven. He inculcated respect for Brahmans as well as Śramaṇas or ascetics of all sects, and was tolerant towards all. The old Vedic or sacrificial religion, *i. e.,* the Karmakâṇḍa, thus received an effectual blow not only at the hands of Buddhists generally, but of Aśoka particularly; so that though attempts were made later on to revive it, as I shall hereafter show, it became obsolete; and it is only rarely that one meets with an Agnihotrin or keeper of the sacred fires, and even the simplest of the old great sacrifices is performed in modern times in but a few and stray instances.

BUDDHISTIC ACCOUNTS.

The Buddhist records give long accounts of Asoka and represent him as one of their great patrons; but they are more or less legendary, and it is difficult to separate the truth from falsehood. Some of their statements, such as that Aśoka visited Buddha's birthplace, are, as we have

---

20 2nd Rock Edict.

21 Cunningham's Corpus Inscr. Ind. plate XVI.; Ind. Ant. Vol. XX. p. 364.

seen, confirmed by the inscriptions. A great council of Buddhist priests is said to have been held at his instance to settle the Buddhistic canon; and though there is nothing improbable in it, still it is rather remarkable that no reference to the event occurs in the inscriptions; and Aśoka does not seem to have interested himself with doctrinal Buddhism so much as to seek its settlement.

SUCCESSORS OF ASOKA.

The names of the successors of Asoka given in the Purânas do not agree. The Vishṇu Purâṇa gives Daśaratha as the name of his grandson, and there are three inscriptions in three caves in the Nagârjuni hills, near Gayâ, in which Daśaratha is represented immediately after his coronation to have dedicated them for the use of the Ajîvaka monks. We have seen that Aśoka dedicated similar caves, which are in the Barâbar hills, for the use of the Ajîvakas. No trace of any other successor of Asoka is found anywhere.

THE SUNGAS AND THE KANVAYANAS.

The dynasty of the Mauryas was uprooted, according to the Purânas, by Pushpamitra or Pushyamitra, who founded the dynasty of the Suṅgas. Pushyamitra is several times alluded to by Patañjali in the Mahâbhâshya, and from the occurrence of his name in a particular passage, I have fixed Patañjali's date to be about 142 B. C. Pushyamitra is represented by the Buddhists to have been their persecutor. It appears from the Mahâbhâshya that he was a staunch adherent of Brahmanism and performed sacrifices. His son Agnimitra is the hero of Kâlidâsa's Mâlavikâgnimitra, in which also there is an allusion to the Aśvamedha performed by Pushyamitra.

---

22 Cunningham's Corpus Inscr. Ind. plate XVI., Ind. Ant. Vol. XX, pp. 364-65.

23 Ind. Ant. Vol. I. p. 299 and ff.; Vol. II. p. 69 and ff.

It will thus appear that he could by no means have been a patron of Buddhism, and the story of his having persecuted them may therefore be true. An inscription on the Buddhistic Stûpa at Bharaut, between Jabalpur and Allahabad, represents the place to have been situated in the dominions of the Suṅgas. Agnimitra was probably his father's viceroy at Vidisâ in eastern Mâlwâ. The Sungas are mentioned as having reigned for 112 years in the Purâṇas. They were followed by the Kâṇvâyanas, the first of whom was Vâsudeva. A duration of forty-five years is assigned to this dynasty.

THE YAVANAS OR BACTRIAN GREEKS.

Long before this time, however, the Yavanas and even the Sakas make their appearance in Indian history. The instances given by Patañjali of the use of the Imperfect to indicate an action well-known to people, but not witnessed by the speaker, and still possible to have been seen by him, are, as is well known, *Arunad Yavanah Saketam: Arunad Yavano Madhamikam* This shows that a certain Yavana or Greek prince had besieged Sâketa or Ayôdhyâ and another place called Madhyamikâ when Patañjali wrote this. The late Dr. Goldstücker identified this Yavana Prince with Menander. He may, however, be identified with Apollodotus, since the coins of both were found near the Jumna, and according to the author of the Periplus, were current at Barygaza (Broach) in the first century A. D. But since Strabo represents Menander to have carried his arms as far as the Jumna, his identification with the Yavana prince is more probable. In another place Patañjali, in the instances to the Sûtra, beginning with *Sûdrânâm,* &c., gives *Saka-yavanam* as an instance of an aggregate

24 Under Pâṇ III. 2, III.

25 Ind. Ant. Vol. VIII. p. 143.

Dvandva which signifies that they were Sûdras and lived beyond the confines of Âryâvarta. I have already alluded to a work in Pâli consisting of dialogues between Milinda and Nâgasena, which is called Milinda-Pañho. Milinda has been identified with Menander, and is represented as a Yavana king whose capital was Śâkala in the Panjâb. The Purâṇas, too, in a passage which is greatly confused, assign the sovereignty of India to Śakas and other foreign tribes. But as the only reliable and definite evidence about these foreign kings is furnished by their coins, we shall now proceed to consider them.

Coins of silver and sometimes of copper have been found in Afghanistan and the Panjâb, even as far eastward as Mathurâ and the Jumna, which bear bilingual legends besides certain emblems characteristic of them. One of these is on the obverse in Greek characters and language, giving the name of the prince as well as his titles; and the other, which is on the reverse, is in the Kharoshṭhî characters, to which I have already drawn attention, and which are written from the right to the left, and in the Pâli or Prâkṛit language. For example, the coins of one of the earlier of these Bactro-Indian princes, Heliocles, contain on the obverse the legend *Basiḷeôs Dikaiou Heliokleous,* which means "of Heliocles, the righteous king," and on the reverse the legend *Mahârâjasa Dhramikasa Heliyakreyasa,* which is the northern Prâkrit for the Sanskrît "Mahârâjasya Dhârmikasya Heliyakreyasya." Now, this Prâkṛit legend could have been used only because the coins were intended to be current in provinces inhabited by Hindus. The princes, therefore, whose coins bear such legends must be considered to have held some province in India. The Kharoshthî characters, as stated before, are used in the rock inscriptions of Aśoka in Afghanistan and on the northern frontiers of the Panjâb. The Kharoshṭhî legend used on the coins, therefore, indicates that in the beginning, the princes who used them must have governed some part of Afghanistan or the Panjâb; and their use was continued even after their possessions extended further eastward. The founder of the Greco-Bactrian monarchy was Diodotus. He was followed by Euthydemus who appears to have been totally unconnected with him. Demetrius, the son of Euthydemus, succeeded him and even in the lifetime of his father carried his arms to India and conquered some territory. Eucratides was his rival and they were at war with each other. But Eucratides in the event succeeded in making himself master of a province in India; and there appear to have been two dynasties or rather factions ruling contemporaneously. To the line of Demetrius belonged Euthydemus II., probably his son, Agathocles and Pantaleon. A prince of the name of Antimachus seems also to have been connected with them.[26] The coins of the first two princes have no Prâkrit legend; those of the next two have it in the Brâhmì or ancient Nâgarî characters, while those of the last have it in the Kharosṭhî. Eucratides was succeeded by Heliocles, his son, who probably reigned from 160 B. C. to 150 B. C. [27] There are bilingual legends on the coins of these. There were other princes who followed these, but whose order has not yet been determined, and the dates, too, have not been settled. Their names are these:—Philoxenus, Lysias, Antialcidas, Theophilus, Amyntas, and Archebius. These and the preceding princes ruled over Bactria and Afghanistan to the south of the Paropamisus, but not over the Panjâb. The names of those who held also the Panjâb and in some cases some of the eastern

26 Percy Gardner's *Coins of the Greek and Scythic kings*, &c. Introduction.

27 Lassent Ind. Alterth. Vol. II. pp. 325-26.

provinces as far as the Jumna, are as follows:—Menander, Apollodotus, Zoilus, Dionysius, Strato, Hippostratus Diomedes, Nicias, Telephus, Hermaeus.[28] Of these the name of Menander occurs, as already stated, in the Pâli work known as the Milindapañho. Milinda is the Indianized form of Menander; and the prince is represented as being very powerful. His capital was Śâkala in the Panjâb.

In the coins of some of these princes the middle word is *apaḍihatasa* corresponding to *Anikêtou* in the Greek legend, as in *Mahârâjasa Apaḍihatasa Philasinasa.* In those of others we have *Jayadharasa* corresponding to *Nikêphorou* in the Greek legend, as in *Mahârâjasa Jayadharasa Antialkiasa.* On the coins of Archebius we have *Mahârâjasa Dhramikasa Jayadharasa Arkhebiyasa,* and on those of others, such as Menander, we have *Tradarasa,* corresponding to the Greek *Sôtêros,* as in *Mahârâjasa, Tradarasa, Menaṁdrasa. Tradarasa* is a corruption of some such word as *trâtârasa* for Sanskrit *trâtuḥ.* On some coins we have *Tejamasa Tâdârasa,* where *tejama* stands for the Greek *Epiphanous,* and means brilliant. Sometimes we have *Mahatasa Jayatasa* after *Mahârâjasa.*

The chronology and the mutual relations of these Greco-Indian kings are by no means clear. Some of the princes reigned in one province contemporaneously with others in other provinces. But it may generally be stated, especially in view of the passage quoted from Patañjali above, and of the tradition alluded to by Kâlidâsa in the Mâlavikâgnimitra, that Pushpamitra's sacrificial horse was captured on the banks of the Sindhu or Indus by Yavana cavalry; it may be concluded that these kings were in possession of parts of India from about the beginning of the second century before Christ

28 *Ib.* Vol. II., Bk. II.

to the arrival of the Śakas whom we shall now proceed to consider.

The Imperial Śakas.

The Śaka coinage is an imitation of the Greco-Bactrian or Greco-Indian coinage, though there are some emblems peculiar to the Sakas. There are two legends, as in the case of the former, one on the obverse in Greek letters, and the other on the reverse in Kharoshthî character and in the Prâkṛit language. Here, too, the mutual relation between the princes, their order of succession, as well as their dates, are by no means clear. Still, from the bi-lingual legends on the coins, we have recently determined the order of the princes, and endeavoured to fix the period when they ruled. The following are the names arranged in the order thus determined:—(i.) Vonones, (ii.) Spalirises, (iii.) Azes I., (iv.) Azilises, (v.) Azes II., and (vi.) Maues. There are coins of two others, *viz.*, Spalahores and his son Spalgadames, who, however, did not succeed to supreme power.[19] Now, one thing to be remarked with reference to these princes is that in the legends on their coins, unlike the Greco Indians, they style themselves *Basileus Basileôn*, corresponding to the Prâkṛit on the reverse *Mahârâjasa Râjarâjasa*. Thus they style themselves "kings of kings," *i. e.*, emperors. They also appropriate the epithet *Mahatasa*, corresponding to the Greek *Megalou*, which we find on the coins of Greek kings. Now, the title "king of kings" cannot in the beginning at least have been an empty boast. The Śakas must have conquered a very large portion of the country before they found themselves in a position to use this imperial title. And we have evidence of the spread of their power. First of all, the era at

19. See the paper written by Mr. Devadatta R. Bhandarkar and published in J. B. B. R, A. S, (pp. 16-25) (1910).

present called Śâlivâhana Śaka was up to about the thirteenth century known by the name of 'the era of the Śaka king of kings' and 'the era of the coronation of the Śaka king.' Now, such an era, bearing the name of the Śaka king that has lasted to the present day, cannot have come to be generally used, unless the Śaka kings had been very powerful, and their dominions extended over a very large portion of the country and lasted for a long time. And we have positive evidence of the extent of their power. Taxila in the Panjâb, and Mathurâ and the surrounding provinces were ruled over by princes who use the title of Kshatrapa or Mahâkshatrapa. So also a very long dynasty of Kshatrapas or Mahâkshatrapas ruled over the part of the country extending from the coast of Kâṭhiawâḍ to Ujjayinî in Mâlwâ. Even the Maratha Country was for some time under the sovereignty of a Kshatrapa, who afterwards became a Mahâkshatrapa. Evidence has been found to consider these Kshatrapas as belonging to the Śaka race, and the very title Kshatrapa, which is evidently the same as the Persian *Khshathrapa*, ordinarily Satrap, shows that these princes were originally of a foreign origin. The coins of the early princes of the Western or Kâṭhiâwâḍ-Mâlwâ Kshatrapas bear on the obverse some Greek characters, and also a few Kharoshṭhî letters, together with a Brâhmî legend on the reverse. And this also points to their connection with the north. These princes give dates on their coins and use them in their inscriptions which have now been considered by all antiquarians to refer to the Śaka era. It is by no means unreasonable therefore to consider these and the Northern Kshatrapas to have been in the beginning at least Viceroys of the Śaka kings, and the Śaka era to have been founded by the most powerful of these kings.

If these considerations have any weight, the Śaka kings, whose names have been given above, founded their power in the latter part of the first century of the Christian era. This goes against the opinion of all scholars and antiquarians who have hitherto written on the subject and who refer the foundation of the Śaka power to about the beginning of the first century before Christ.[30].

NORTHERN KSHATRAPAS.

The names of Northern Kshatrapas found on coins and in inscriptions are Zeionises, Kharamostis; Liaka and Patika who bore the surname Kusulaka and governed the North-Western Panjâb at Taxila; and Râjuvula and his son Śoḍâsa who held power at Mathurâ.[31] The names of Liaka and Patika are found in a copperplate inscription in which the foundation of a monastery and the placing of a relic of Śâkyamuni are recorded.[32] Inscriptions have been discovered at Mathurâ and Morâ in Rajputana,[33] whice are dated in the reign of Śoḍâsa. There was also found a Lion pillar at Mathurâ on which there is an inscription in which the names of the mother of Śoḍâsa, his father Râjuvula, and other relatives are given, as well as those of the allied Kshatrapas, *viz.*, Patika of Takshaśilâ and Miyika.[34] The names of two

---

30 See D. R. Bhandarkar's paper referred to before, for the whole argument. Many circumstances have been brought forward, all of which point to the conclusion which we have arrived at, and thus render it highly probable. The objection against it, based on the style of the coins, has also been considered.

31 Numismatic Chronicle for 1890, pp. 125-129; Percy Gardner's Coins of Greek and Scythic Kings of India.

32 Ep. Ind. Vol. IV., p. 54 ff.

33 Cunningham's Arch. Rep. Vol. III., p. 30, and Vol. XX., p. 49, and Ep. Ind. Vol. II., p. 199.

34 Jour. R. A. S. 1894, p. 533 ff.

other Kshatrapas, Hagâna and Hagâmasha,[35] have been discovered. The coins of Zeionises and Kharamostis, and some of Râjuvula, bear on the obverse a Greek legend and on the reverse one in Kharoshṭhî characters, thus showing their close connection with their Śaka masters. Some of Râjuvula and those of Śoḍâsa, Hagâna and Hagâmasha have a Brâhmî legend only. Râjuvula uses high-sounding imperial titles on some of his coins, whence it would appear that he made himself independent of his overlord. The date of his son Śoḍâsa is 72,[36] equivalent, according to our view, to 150 A. D. It would thus appear that the Satraps who governed Mathurâ and the eastern portion of the Śaka empire declared themselves, independent some time before 150 A. D., while those who governed north-western Panjâb at Taxila, and consequently were nearer to their sovereign lords, acknowledged their authority till 78 Saka or 150 A. D., as is evident from Patika's mention of Moga, who has been identified with the Saka Emperor Maues, in the Taxila copperplate inscription referred to before.

KSHATRAPAS OF KÂṬHIÂWÂḌ-MÂLWÂ.

Silver coins of the Kshatrapas of Kâṭhiâwâḍ or Surâshṭra and Mâlwâ have been found in large numbers in those provinces. The latest find was in the rock-cells and temples to the south of the Uparkot, a fortress of Junâgaḍh in Kâṭhiâwâḍ, which consisted of twelve hundred coins of different kings.[37] On the obverse there is a bust of the reigning prince very often with the date, and on the reverse there is in the centre an emblem which has the appearance of a Stûpa with a wavy line below

35 *Ibid.* p. 549, and Cunningham's Coins of Anc. Ind., p. 87.

36 Ep. Ind., Vol. VII., p. 199, and Vol. IV., p. 55, n. 2.

37 Jour. B. B. R. A. S., Vol. XX., p. 201.

and the sun and the crescent of the moon at the top. Round this central emblem is the legend giving the name of the prince with that of his father and the title Kshatrapa or Mahâkshatrapa, in Brâhmî or old Devanâgarî character and in mixed Sanskrit and Prâkṛit. The first prince of this dynasty was Chashṭana, son of Ghsamotika. There are Greek letters on the obverse of his coins which have but recently been read and found to contain the name of the prince. The legend on the reverse is *Râjño Mahâkshatrapasa Ghsamotikaputrasa Chashṭanasa.* The coins of this prince do not bear dates; but Chashtana is mentioned by Ptolemy as Tiastenes, a prince reigning at Ozênê or Ujjayinî. And from this and other circumstances his date has been determined to be about 132 A.D. The name Chashṭana and Ghsamotika are evidently foreign and not Indian. Chashṭana had a large number of successors, some of whom are called Kshatrapas only and others Mahâkshatrapas. There are others again who were Kshatrapas in the early part of their career and Mahâkshatrapas in the later. The former was evidently an inferior title and showed that the bearer of it was a dependent prince while a Mahâkshatrapa held supreme power. There are inscriptions also in which the names of some of these princes are mentioned. In one at Junâgadh dated 72, Rudradâman's minister Suviśâkha, a Pahlava, son of Kulaipa, is represented to have re-constructed the dam that had broken away of the lake Sudarśana. In it Rudradâman is spoken of as having been at war with Śâtakarṇi, the lord of the Dekkan, and subjected to his sway a good many provinces to the north of Surâshṭra. There is another inscription bearing the date 103 found at Guṇḍâ, in the Jâmnagar State, in which Rudrabhûti is represented as having dug a tank and constructed it in the reign of the Kshatrapa Rudrasiṁha, son of Mahâkshatrapa Rudradâman, grandson of Kshatrapa Jayadâman, and great grandson of Mahâkshatrapa Chashṭana.[38] A third found at Jasdan in Kâthiawâd and dated 127, while Rudrasena was ruling, records the construction of a Sattra or a feeding-house for travellers by one whose name appears to be Mânasasagara, and who was the son of Praṇâthaka and grandson of Khara.[39] The genealogy of Rudrasena that is given is, that he was [the son] of Rudrasiṁha, grandson of Rudradâman, grandson of the son of Jayadâman, and great grandson of the son of Chashṭana. Another inscription at Junâgadh of the grandson of Jayadâman represents some sort of gift in connection with those who had become Kevalis, *i. e.*, perfect individuals, according to Jainas. And the last that I have to notice is that found at Mulwâsar in Okhâmandala which refers itself to the reign of Rudrasena and bears the date 122.[40]

The following is a complete list of the Kshatrapa princes with the dates occurring on the coins and in the inscriptions:—

I. *Mahâkshatrapas.*	II. *Kshatrapas.*
1. Chashtana	1. Chashṭana.
	2. Jayadâman, son of Chashṭana.
2. Rudradâman son of Jayadâman, 72.	3. Dâmaghsada son of Rudradâman.
3. Dâmaghsada son of Rudradâman	4. Rudrasiṁha son of Rudradâman, 102, 110, 112.

38 Bhownagar Coll. of Incr., p. 22.

39 Ib. p. 22 facs. and Jour. B. B. R. A. S., Vol. III, p. 234.

40 Bhownagar Coll. of Incr. p. 7 and p. 23; see also Jour. R. A. S., April 1899, ff. 380 ff.

4. Rudrasiṁha son of Rudradâman, 101, 103, 105, 106, 108, 109, 110, 113, 114, 115, 116, 118.
5. Jîvadâman son of Dâmaghsada, 119, 120.
6. Rudrasena son of Rudrasiṁha, 122, 125, 130, 131, 133, 134, 135, 136, 138, 139, 140, 142, 144.
7. Saṁghadâman son of Rudrasiṁha, 144, 149.
8. Dâmasena son of Rudrasiṁha, 145, 150, 151, 152, 153, 154, 155, 156, 157, 158.
9. Dâmajadaśrî son of Rudrasena.
10. Yaśodâman son of Dâmasena, 160, 161.
11. Vijayasena son of Dâmasena, 161, 163, 164, 165, 166, 167, 168, 170, 171, 172.
12. Dâmajadaśrî son of Dâmaśena, 172, 173, 174, 175, 176, 177.
13. Rudrasena son of Vîradâman, 177, 178, 180, 182, 183, 185, 186, 187, 188, 189, 190, 191, 194, 197.

5. Satyadâman son Damaghsada.
6. Rudrasena son of Rudrasiṁha, 121.
7. Pṛithvîsena son of Rudrasena, 144.
8. Dâmjadaśrî son of Rudrasena, 154, 155.
9. Vîradâman son of Dâmasena, 158, 159, 160.
10. Yaśodâman son of Dâmasena, 160.
11. Vijayasena son of Dâmasena, 160.
12. Visvasimha son of Rudrasena, 197, 198, 199, 200.

14. Viśvasiṁha son of Rudrasena, 200.

15. Bhartṛidâman son of Rudrasena, 203, 204, 205, 206, 207, 209, 210, 211, 212, 213, 214, 215, 217, 220?

16. Svâmi-Rudrasena son of Svâmi-Mahâkshatrapa Rudradâman, 270, 271, 272, 273, 288, 290, 292, 293, 294, 296, 298, 300.

17. Svâmi-Siṁhasena sister's son of Svâmi-Rudrasena, 304.

18. Svâmi-(Rudra?) sena son of Svâmi-Siṁhasena.

19. Svâmi-Rudrasiṁha son of Svâmi-Mahâkshatrapa Satyasena, 310.

13. Bhartridâman son of Rudrasena, 200, 201, 202, 204.

14. Visvasena son of Bhartṛidâman, 215, 216, 217, .218, 219, 220, 221, 222, 223, 224, 225, 226.

15. Rudrasiṁha son Svâmi Jîvadâman, 226, 227, 228, 229, 230, 231, 232, 234, 238.

16. Yasodâman son of Rudrasiṁha, 238, 239, 240, 241, 242, 243, 244, 245, 249, 252, 253, 254.

Though the Kshatrapas occupied a subordinate position, they issued coins in their name, and from that it would appear that they were put in charge of a separate province. Probably the Mahâkshatrapas reigned at the capital, whether it was Ujjayinî as in Chashṭana's time, or any other town, and the Kshatrapas in Kâṭhiâwâḍ.

THE RULE OF SUCCESSION AMONG THE KSHATRAPAS AND THE IMPERIAL ŚAKAS.

It will be seen that Rudradâman, the second in list I. was succeeded by his son Dàmaghsada, and he by his brother Rudrasimha and not by his son Satyadâman, who was only a Kshatrapa under his uncle. After the two brothers, their sons became Mahâkshatrapas successively; and after Rudrasena, the eldest son of Rudrasiṁha, his two brothers held the supreme power one after another, and two sons of Rudrasena were only Kshatrapas under their uncle. Similarly, three sons of Dâmasena (Nos. 10, 11 and 12) reigned one after another. The position of Kshatrapa under the Mahâkshatrapa was occupied by the brother of the latter, as in the case of No. 4 in list II; in the absence of the brother, by the elder brother's son, and in his absence, his own son. After the brothers had been in power successively, their sons, beginning with those of the eldest, got possession of the throne, as in the case of Nos. 6, 7, 8, 9, 10, 11 and 12 in list I. Thus, according to the custom of this dynasty, the rightful heir to the throne was the next brother, and after the brothers, the sons, in the order of their father's seniority. Dr. Bühler conjectures the existence of a similar custom among the northern Kshatrapas from the fact of Kharoshta's bearing the title of *Yuvarâja,* while his brother Śoḍâsa was a reigning Kshatrapa.[41] But it can be distinctly traced among the imperial Śakas. For, while the coins of Vonones represent him in Greek characters on the obverse as "King of kings," they show on the reverse in Kharoshṭhî characters that his brother Sphalahores held power under him, as the brother of a Mâlwâ Mahâkshatrapa did under the latter. On other coins we have Spalgadames, the son of Sphalahores, associated on the reverse with Vonones on the

41 *Jour. R. A. S.*, 1894, p. 532.

obverse. This Spalgadames is again connected on the obverse with Spalirises, who is styled "the king's brother." There are other coins on which Spalirises appears in both the Greek and Kharoshṭhî legends as "King of kings." Still others we have, on which he, as supreme sovereign, is associated with Azes on the reverse in Kharoshṭhî characters. There is one coin described by Sir A. Cunningham, in which Azes on the reverse is associated with Vonones on the obverse. No coin has been discovered on which Vonones appears on the reverse in Kharoshṭhí characters. All this shows that Vonones was the first supreme sovereign; that Azes was dependent first on him and afterwards on Spalirises; and consequently that Spalirises succeeded Vonones; and that the *Mahârâja*, or Great King,' whose brother Spalirises is represented to be, must have been Vonones. The latter had another brother named Spalahores; but since he is not represented as an independent sovereign on the obverse in Greek characters on any coin, and instead of him his son's name is associated with Vonones, he must have died during the life-time of the latter, and Spalirises, another brother, assumed Spalahores' position, and Spalgadames was at one time subordinate to him, and also at another time directly to Vonones. Subsequently Spalirises, being Vonones' brother, obtained supreme power after his death. The phrase *Mahârâjabhrâtâ*, or "king's brother," is used pointedly to indicate the right of the person to be crown prince and subsequently to be successor. The prevalence of this custom among the imperial Śakas shows that Mahâkshatrapas and Kshatrapas of India were intimately connected with them, *i. e.*, derived their authority originally from them and were Sakas.

42 Percy Gardiner's *Coins of Greek and Scythic Kings*, pp. 98-102 and rum. Chr., 1890 p. 138.

FORTUNES OF THE KSHATRAPA FAMILY OF KATHIÂWAD-MALWA.

Chashtana was at first a Kshatrapa and then a Mahâkshatrapa, probably because he first acknowledged the supremacy of his Saka overlord and afterwards assumed independence. Jayadâman, his son, was a Kshatrapa only; and the reason appears to have been the same as that given by me in the "Early History of the Dekkan," *viz.*, that Gotamîputra and Pulumâyi invaded Ujjayinî and deprived him of supreme power. Rudradâman, his son, then acquired his lost kingdom and assumed the title of Mahâkshatrapa. After Rudradâman the succession is regular up to Bhatṛidaman, *i. e.*, till about 226 Śaka, or 304 A. D. Then up to 270 Śaka, or rather 288, *i. e.*, for about 62 years, we have no Mahâkshatrapa. This must have been due to a prince or princes of some other family having established their sway over Mâlwâ; and we have an inscription at Sâñchi of Vâsushka, Bazdeo, or Vâsudeva, who belonged to the Kushana family to be mentioned hereafter, bearing the date 78. If the interpretation of the date of the princes of that family given in the paper referred to above and explained below is correct this corresponds to 278 Saka. Very likely, therefore, Kanishka, the first or most famous prince of the family, whose dates range from 205 to 228 Saka, subjugated Mâlwâ about the year 226 Śaka, and he and his successors retained possession of the province till about 288 Śaka. The earliest date of the restored Mahâkshatrapa is 270, but his coins are continuous only for four years. Then there is a gap of 15 years between 273 and 288, which shows that his power was not firmly established in 270, and that he was driven out again in

43 Second Ed., pp. 28-29.

44 Epigraphia Indica, Vol. II, p. 369.

273. But a short time after, the Kushanas were humbled by the rising Guptas; and this last circumstance must have been availed of by the Mahâkshatrapas to regain their power, which they did in 288 Śaka. It was, however, not long before the rising power turned its attention to Mâlwâ also and the Mahâkshatrapa dynasty retained its regained sovereignty for about 22 or 23 years only and was finally exterminated by the Guptas in 310 or 311 Śaka, *i. e.*, 388 or 389 A. D. There must have been some minor revolution before this, when a prince of the name of Iśvaradatta made himself a Mahâkshatrapa and issued coins dated in the first and second years of his reign. He does not appear to have belonged to this dynasty.

KSHATRAPAS AND SÂTAVÂHANAS IN THE DEKKAN.

From an inscription at Junnar and others in the Nâsik and Kârli caves, we see that the sovereignty of Satraps was established over Mahârâshṭra also. But we find the name of one Mahâkshatrapa only, *viz.*, Nahapâna, and after him we have no names of Satraps that may be supposed to have ruled over the country, and find instead that the princes of the Śâtavâhana or Śâlivâhana race were in possession of Maharashtra. An inscription in one of the caves at Nasik speaks of Gotamîputra Śâtakarṇi as having beaten the Śakas, the Yavanas and the Pahlavas, and left no remnant of the race of Khakharâta. In the inscriptions, Nahapâna, also named Kshaharâta, which is but another form of Khakharâta. Gotamîputra therefore must be understood to have destroyed the lineal successor of Nahapâna. Again, in the inscription alluded to above he is also represented to have re-established the power of the Sâtavâhana family. Thus, the Sâtavâhanas were in possession of the Mahârâshṭra before the Śakas invaded the country. The principal seat of the family was Dhanakaṭaka, but the younger princes ruled over the Dekkan and had Paiṭhaṇ for their capital. The earliest prince of this dynasty whose name is found in the inscriptions was Kṛishṇa. The name of one still earlier Simuka Sâta vâhana also occurs, but not as a prince reigning at the time. Kṛishṇa was followed by Śâtakarṇi. Śâtakarṇi's successors must have been in possession of the country till the latter part of the first century of the Christian era, when the Śakas established their power. These, however, were driven out of the country by Gotamîputra, and we have the names of Pulumâyi, Yajñaśrî Śâtakarni, Chatushparna Sâtakarṇi and Maḍharî-putra Śakasena, the successors of Gotamîputra, in the inscriptions in the caves and on the coins found at Bassein and Kolhapur, and not that of any Kshatrapa. So that the Śakas ruled over the Dekkan for about one generation only.

The Sâtavâhana dynasty is mentioned in the Purâṇas under the name of the Ândhrabhṛityas, and most of the names given above, Simuka, the founder, Krishṇa Śâtakarṇi, Gotamîputra Śâtakarṇi, Puḷumâyi and Yajñasrî Śâtakarṇi occur in the genealogy there given. The names of Chatushparṇa add Śakasena, however, do not occur. This dynasty is represented in the Purâṇas to have succeeded the Kâṇvâyanas. But they do not appear to have held sway in Northern India. Nahapâna's dates occurring in the inscriptions of his son-in-law, Ushavadâta, are 40, 41, and 42, and that occurring in the inscription at Junnar of his minister Ayama is 46. On the supposition that the era is Śaka, these are 118, 119, 120 and 124 A. D. Puḷumâyi is represented as ruling at Paiṭhaṇ by Ptolemy, as he has represented Chashṭana to be the king of Ujjayinî. They were therefore contemporaries. Hence the Śakas or Satraps were driven away from Mahârâshṭra between 124 and 132 A. D. They, however, as has been shown before, ruled over Surâshṭra and Mâlwâ with some intermissions till 389 A. D. In the earlier years Nâhapâna is called a mere Kshatrapa in the inscriptions; but in the Junnar inscription of his minister he is called a Mahâkshatrapa, which shows that like Chashṭana he at first acknowledged the sovereign power of his Śaka lord in the north, and then assumed independence.

THE INDO-PARTHIANS OR PAHLAVAS.

In the north, the Kshatrapas and the Śaka emperors soon lost their power. They were succeeded by the Indo-Parthian or Pahlava kings. Their names, determined from coins, are as follows :—

1. Gondophares.
2. Abdagases, nephew of Gondophares.
3. Orthagnes.
4. Arsakes.
5. Pakores.
6. Sanabares.

An inscription of Gondophares bearing date 103 has been discovered at Takht-i-Bahi, to the north-east of Peshâwâr. This is represented as the 26th year of his reign, and if the date refers to the Śaka era, and is equivalent to 181 A. D., Gondophares began to reign in 155 A. D. His coins are found in Seistan, Kandahar and even in Western Panjâb. He had probably dispossessed the Śakas of their western provinces about the time his reign began, but they continued to hold those to the east as we know from the date 78, equivalent to 156 A. D. of Moga. The date in Takht-i-Bahi inscription has been referred to the Vikrama era and supposed to correspond to 47 A. D., and Gondophares' accession to the throne placed in 21 A. D. A story that for the first time became current in the fourth century in Christian countries in the west represents St. Thomas to have visited Gondophares and suffered martyrdom, and if regarded as true it confirms the date 21 as that of his accession. But if such a prince was remembered in the fourth century, much more reasonable is it to suppose that he was not removed from it by so many as three hundred years, but only by about 150 at the most, and probably less than that. The coins of these kings have Greek legends on the obverse and Kharoshṭhî in the Prâkṛit dialect, as in the case of the Śakas and the Greeks. But they use high titles like the Śakas. On some of Gondophares' coins we have in the Greek legend *Basileus Basileôn Megalou Gundophernou,* and in the Kharoshṭhî *Mahârâjasa râjarâjasa Devatrâtasa Gudapharasa,* meaning 'of Gudaphara the great king, king of kings, protected by the gods. On his coins all the high-sounding epithets, one of which only was used by his predecessors, are found, such as *Apratihata Dhramika* equivalent to *Dhârmika, Mahata,* and *Trâdata* equivalent to *trâtuh.* Some of his coins have not the Kharoshṭhî legend at all, but only Greek—which probably shows that he added Indian provinces to his dominions after he had reigned for some time. The legends on the coins of his successors are more or less corrupt. This, as well as the fact of the use of all the magniloquent epithets noticed above, shows that his dynasty succeeded those I have already noticed. The most important of these Parthian princes was Gondophares, and he held possession of a large extent of country ; but he does not seem to have penetrated to the east of the Panjâb. The territories ruled over by his successors were much narrower.

THE KUSHÂNAS.

After the Indo-Parthian or Pahlava dynasty and perhaps in the beginning, contemporaneous with it, we have another that gave itself the name of *Kushâna.* The Princes of this family known to us by name are as follows:—

1. Kujula-Kadphises.
2. Wema-Kadphises.
3. Kanishka.
4. Huvishka.
5. Vâsudeva or Vâsushka.

Copper coins of a prince whose imperial titles are given thereon, but whose name does not occur, are found in large numbers in the Panjâb, Kandahar, and the Kabul valley, and even in Mâlwâ. There are a few silver coins also. He probably belonged to this family and preceded Wema-Kadphises. The last three princes in the above list are noticed in the Râjâtaraṇginî and are represented as belonging to the Turushka race; that is to say, they were Turks. And the dress, especially the cap, and the features of the royal figures on their coins appear Turkish. I have already observed that some of the Greek kings reigned contemporaneously with princes of the later dynasties. Some coins of Kujula-Kadphises, on the obverse of which is the name of the Greek prince Hermaeus, have on the reverse the name of Kujula-Kapsa or Kasa without high-sounding titles. This would show that he was subordinate to Hermaeus and also that some Greek prince continued to reign somewhere while the Śakas and the Indo-Parthians had supreme power. There are, however, other coins on which the name of Hermaeus does not occur, which indicates that he afterwards acquired independence. But it was his successor Wema-Kadphises who appears to have conquered a large extent of the country and risen to supreme power, as imperial titles appear on his coins, while they do not on those of Kujula-Kadphises. The same conclusion is pointed to by the fact that his coins are not merely confined to the Kabul valley and the Panjâb as those of Kujula, but are found eastward as far as Gorakhpur and Ghazipur and along the line of railway from Allahabad to Jabalpur. Some of his coins have in the Greek legend *Basileus Basileôn Megas Wema Kadphises*, and in the Kharoshṭhî legend *Mahârâjasa râjadhirâjasa Sarvaloga-isvarasa Mahisvarasa Hima-Kathpisasa tradata*, *i. e.*, 'Hima Kadphises the great king, king of kings, the sovereign lord of all people, devotee of Maheśvara and Saviour.' Several much later kings are called *Maheś-varas, i. e.*, devotees of Maheśvara or Śiva, or belonging to the sect of Maheśvaras. Wema-Kadphises seems to be so spoken of on his coins; and that he was a worshipper of Śiva is shown also by the emblem of Nandin on the reverse of his coins accompanied by a human figure which, because it holds a trident in its right arm, must represent Śiva. He was the first of all the kings we have noticed who used gold coinage and was in this respect followed by his successors.

THE LAST THREE KUSHÂNAS.

The three next kings call themselves Kushanas on their coins. The royal figure on them has a dress similar to that on those of Wema-Kadphises. But these three Kushânas seem to have struck an independent path for themselves in respect of their coins, which may perhaps point to their constituting an independent family. The legend is only one in Greek letters. On some coins of Kanishka it is in the Greek language also and reads, *Basileôs Basileôn Kanheshkou, i. e.*, 'Kaniskha, king of kings.' On the majority of his coins, however, and on those of his successors it is in Greek letters, and perhaps in the Turkish language, and reads *Shaonano Shao Kanheski Kushano*, *Shaonao Shao Huvishki Kushano*, *i. e.*, 'the Shah (king) of Shahs, Kanhiska Kushana, &c. The emblems on the reverse are figures of deities from the Greek, Persian, and Brahmanic pantheon and of Buddha. By the side of these figures their names also are given in Greek characters. Thus we have Salênê, Hêlios, and Herakeo; Mihiro = Mahira, Mazdohano = Mazdaonho; Skando, Mahaseno, Komaro, Bizago, which last is equivalent to Viśâkha, Boddo = Buddho, and Saka Mana Boddo Sâkya Muni Buddha.[45] Thus these Turkish kings paid an equal respect to the gods of all these four religions. But the figures of Buddha in the sitting or meditative and the standing posture, occur on coins of Kanishka only. This may be regarded as evidence of the truth of what the northern Buddhists say as to Kanishka being their patron. In his time and under his patronage a council of priests was held to settle the canon again, and it was at this time that Buddhism, which had gradually been veering towards the Mahâyâna form, had that character definitely impressed upon it.

THEIR DATES.

There are a great many inscriptions dated in the reigns of these three kings. They are chiefly dedications of Buddhistic and Jaina objects of worship for the use of the people, and occur principally at Mathurâ. As stated before, there is one inscription bearing the date 78 and referring itself to the reign of Vâsudeva at Sâñchi. There is not a single Brahmanic

45 Percy Gardner, p. 129, pp. 129 ff.; Cunningham Num. Chron. 1892, pp. 63 ff.

inscription. The dates vary from 5 in the reign of Kanishka to 98 in the reign of Vâsudeva. Most scholars and antiquarians, a few years ago, believed Kanishka to be the founder of the Śaka era, but the faith of some has been shaken. On this supposition the dates mentioned above run from 83 A. D. to 176 A. D. But according to all accounts, the Guptas succeeded the Kushanas; like the latter, and unlike the previous rulers, they issued a gold coinage, which is a close imitation of that of the latter. The forms of letters in the inscriptions of the Kushanas appear to belong to a later period. For these reasons I have always believed Kanishka to have flourished later than the first century of the Christian era, and we have recently considered the whole question and come to the conclusion formerly stated that one of the Imperial Saka kings founded the Śaka era. Kanishka between whom and the Śaka founder of the Śaka era came the other Saka princes, the Indo-Parthians, and Wema-Kadphises, reigned much later. The practice of omitting hundreds in dates has long existed in that part of India; and, in consideration of the fact that an inscription found at Mathurâ, which though the name of the prince is omitted, contains titles used by the Kushanas and bears the date 290 and some units which are not distinct, the conclusion is reasonable that the dates in the inscription of these three Kushana princes are abbreviated by the omission of two hundreds. These dates must be referred to the Śaka era, and will thus run from 205 Śaka to 298 Śaka, *i. e.*, 283 A. D. to 376 A. D. And the period here assigned to the Kushana princes agrees

---

46 Vienna Oriental Journal, Vol. X., pp. 171-2. The theory of the omission of hundreds may perhaps seem to be out of the way; but even if it is disregarded, the period when these Kushana rulers lived could not have been far removed from that assigned to them. The whole question requires to be thoroughly re-considered.

with all that is known of them and their relations with other princes. The chronology of the previous dynasties also has been arranged in a manner consistent with it, and there is nothing against it, except numismatic theories, which, however, in consideration of the many types available for the princes of these dynasties and the play of fancy, such as is presented to our view by the coins of the last three Kushana princes, cannot be rigidly adhered to

PREDOMINANCE OF EARLY BUDDHISM AND OF THE PRÂKRIT DIALECTS DURING THE PERIOD GONE OVER.

Thus from about the beginning of the second century before Christ, to about the end of the fourth century after, princes of foreign races were prominent in the history of India and ruled sometimes over a large portion of the country up to the limits of Mahârâshṭra. The names of no Hindu princes appear in inscriptions or on coins during this period, except in Mahârâshṭra, where, as we have seen, the Śâtavâhanas drove the foreigners and governed the country, and in the south to which the foreigners did not penetrate. During this period it is the religion of Buddha alone that has left prominent traces, and was professed by the majority of the people. The vestiges of the time are Stûpas or hemispherical structures purporting to contain a relic of Buddha or of saints, and monasteries, and temples containing smaller Stûpas or Chaityas. These Stûpas or Chaityas were the objects of worship amongst the Buddhists. And wherever there is a stupendous Stûpa we find sculptures representing Buddhistic sacred objects, such as the Bodhi or Pippala and other trees under

47 See D. R. Bhandarkar's paper referred to before (pp. 26 ff.).

which Sâkyamuni and the previous Buddhas attained perfection, wheels representing, metaphorically, the *Dharmachakra,* or wheel of righteousness, which Buddha turned, and so forth. There are sculptures also representing events in the previous births of Buddha, about which many stories were current, and which we now find in the so-called Jâtaka literature. Now, the remains of Vihâras, Chaityagṛihas, and Stûpas are found in all parts of the country, including Afghanistan. Some of them contain inscriptions also recording the gifts of public or private individuals. These gifts are the big structures themselves, as well as smaller parts thereof, such as railings, pillars, and sculptures, and sometimes land or deposits of money for the maintenance of the priests. Now, from the inscriptions recording these gifts, we find the position of the persons who made them. The remains of two great Stûpas exist in Central India at Sâñchi in the Bhopal territory, and Bharaut between Jabalpur and Allahabad, near the Sattan Station of the Railway. From the form of characters existing in the inscriptions found in them, the ages of the Stûpas can be approximately determined. That at Bharaut was begun about the middle of the third century before Christ, and continued to be added to till about the end of the second century. The Sâñchi Stûpa was probably first constructed about the same time; and it continued to be an object of adoration and additional gifts till about the eighth century of the Christian era. The donors, as recorded in these two places, were oftentimes the Buddhist monks and nuns themselves, but the names of a great many lay-followers also occur. Thus we have gifts from Grahapatis or householders or landholders; Śeṭṭhis or Śeths, who occupied a prominent position in a town or village; simple traders, who are called Vâṇija or Vâṇika; Râjalipikâras or royal scribes; Lekhakas or professional writers; and even Kâmikas, or ordinary workmen. In the cave-temples in Mahârâshṭra, which began to be excavated about the middle of the first century before Christ, and continued to increase in number and to have additional decorations till the end of the second century after, and were the objects of adoration and resort up to about the end of the ninth century, we find, among the donors, princes and chiefs who called themselves Mahâbhojas and Mahâraṭhis, Naigamas or merchants, Suvarṇakâras or goldsmiths, Vardhakas or carpenters, Dhânyakaśrenis or guilds of corn-dealers, and Gṛihapatis or ordinary householders. There are some Śakas and Yavanas also amongst them. The great cave-temple at Kârli was originally excavated by Bhûtapâla, the Śet of Vaijayantî; the lion-pillar in the court in front was scooped out by a Mahârathi named Agimitra. One of the cave-temples at Nâsik was the gift of Gotamî, mother of Gotamîputra Śâtakarṇi and grandmother of Puḷumâyi. A monastery there was the benefaction of Ushavadâta, son-in-law of Nahapâna, who deposited sums of money also with the guilds of weavers and another guild at Govardhana near Nâsik, out of the interest on which new garments were to be given to the priests in the rainy season. Such money-benefactions were also made by private individuals, as recorded in the inscriptions at Nâsik and Kânheri. The period that we have been speaking of has left no trace of a building or sculpture devoted to the use of the Brahmanic religion. Of course, Brahmanism existed, and it was probably, during the period, being developed into the form which it assumed in later times. The large but unfortunately mutilated inscription at Nânâghâṭ, which is to be referred to the second half of the first century before Christ, opens with an invocation to Dharma, Indra, Saṁkarshaṇa and Vâsudeva, and seems to speak of the Dakshiṇâ or fees given by a royal lady for the performance of several Brahmanic sacrifices. Gifts were made even by princes and chiefs to Brahmans. Ushavadâta the son-in-law of Nahapâna, was a patron of both Brahmans and Buddhists. Some of the Satraps of Surâshṭra and Mâlwâ were probably adherents of Brahmanism, as is indicated by their adoption of the name of the god, Rudra as a component of their own names. Wema-Kadphises was as we have seen, a worshipper of Siva. In the South, we have inscriptions of Śivaskandavarman, a ruler of Kâñchî, of Hârîtiputra Sâtakarṇi and of a king of Banayâsî which are to be referred to the early part of the third century after Christ, and in which grants of land to Brahmans are recorded But the religion certainly does not occupy a prominent position, and Buddhism was followed by the large mass of the people from princes down to the humble workman. Another peculiarity of the period was the use of the Pâli or the current Prâkṛit language in inscriptions. Even the Brahmanic inscription at Nânâghâṭ and those in the south just noticed are composed in this dialect. Sanskrit was the language of learned Brahmans and Prâkṛit of ordinary people of all castes. The use of the latter therefore, indicates a greater deference for these people than for Brahmanic learning. The inscriptions in Kâṭhiâwâḍ, however, of the reigns of the Satrap kings are in Sanskrit and those of Ushavadâta are in mixed Sanskrit and Prâkṛit. But in the middle of the fourth century, the whole scene changes, and we now proceed to the consideration of the events which it presents to our view.

---

48 Ep. Ind. Vol. VI. p. 84 ff. and Vol. I. p. 2 ff. Ind. Ant. Vol. XXV, p. 28.

CHANGE OF SCENE—THE GUPTAS.

I have already observed that the Guptas succeeded the Kushânas. The first prince was named Gupta, and his son was Ghaṭctkacha, both of whom are styled *Mahârâja.* Ghatotkacha's son was Chandragupta I., who is styled *Mahârâjâdhirâja,* of "King or kings" in the inscriptions. It was during the time of this king that the power of the Guptas must have begun to rise. But his son Samudragupta seems to have been one of the most powerful princes of this dynasty. There is a long inscription describing his exploits on the same pillar at Allahabad, which contains inscriptions of Asoka. There he is called *Parâkramâṅka,* which title is also to be found in other inscriptions as well as on his coins. He is represented to have conquered and re-established in their dominions Mahendra, king of Kosala, Vyâghrarâja, king of Mahâkântâra, Maṇṭarâja of Keraḷa and many other kings of Dakshiṇâpatha, to have rooted out kings reigning in Aryâvarta of the names of Rudra-deva, Matila, Nâgadatta Chandravarman, Gaṇapatinâga Nâgasena, Achyutanandin, Balavarman, and others, and probably established his supremacy over their provinces; reduced to submission the chiefs of the forest regions ; exacted tribute from and subjected to his power the kings of Samataṭa, Dâvaka, Kâmarûpa, Nepâla, Karṭripura, and other countries on the borders, and tribes of Mâlavas, Ârjunâyanas, Yaudheyas, Mâdrakas, Âbhîras, Prârjunas Sanakânîkas, and Kâkakharaparikas ; to have re-established certain royal families which had lost their king doms ; and to have formed alliances with Daivaputra Shâhi Shâhânushâhi, princes of the Śaka and Muruṇḍa ribes, and with the Saiṁhaḷakas, who propitiated him with presents. There is an inscription referring itself

49 Dr. Fleet's Insc. Early Gupta Kings., No. 1.

to his reign found at Eraṇ in the Sâgar district, which bears evidence to the fact that his dominions extended up to that district. He was followed by Chandragupta II., one of whose inscriptions dated in the year 82, is found at Udayagiri, near Bhilsâ, in Eastern Mâlwâ. It must here be remarked that the Guptas established an era of their own as to the initial date of which there were long controversies among antiquarians, though it was given by Alberuni, the Arabic traveller, as corresponding to 242 of the Śaka era. But the question is now settled. Alberuni's statement has been found to be correct and the first year of the Gupta era fell in 318-19 A. D. Chandragupta's date 82, therefore, corresponds to 400 A. D. Another inscription of the same occurs at Mathurâ, showing that the Guptas had extended their power to that province which was subject before to the Kushanas. There is one more at Gaḍhwâ, near Allahabad, dated in the year 88, corresponding to 406 A. D., another at Sâñchi, dated 93, corresponding to 411 A. D., and a third at Udayagiri, which bears no date. These inscriptions show that the dominions of the Guptas embraced in the time of Chandragupta II., the whole of the North-Western Provinces and Mâlwâ and the Central Provinces. In the Udayagiri inscription which bears no date that monarch is represented as " wonderful sunlike brilliance" itself, and Saba Vîrasena, who was his minister and a native of Pâtaliputra as having accompanied the king in his career of conquest (*lit.* "the king whose object was to conquer the whole world") to the place *i. e.*, Udayagiri, or the region in which it was situated. The conquest of Mâlwâ by Chandragupta thus alluded to in this inscription took place before 400 A. D.

50 *Ib.* No. 2.
51 *Ib.* No. 3.
52 *Ib.* No. 4.
53 *Ib.* Nos. 5, 6, 7.

the date of the first Udayagiri inscription. The latest date of the Ujjayinî Mahâkshatrapas is, as we have seen, 310 Śaka or 388 A. D. These were exterminated by him in that year or about a year after, a conclusion which follows from the facts that the Kshatrapas issued new coins nearly every year, and there is no issue later than 310 Śaka. Chandragupta II. was followed by Kumâragupta. There are six inscriptions of his reign,—two at Gaḍhwâ, one at Bilsâḍ, Eṭâ district, North-Western Provinces, one at Mankuwâr, Allahabad district, one at Mathurâ, and one at Mandasor in Western Mâlwâ. One Gaḍhwâ inscription bears the date 98, corresponding to 416 A. D., that at Bilsâḍ, the year 96, corresponding to 414 A. D., that at Mathurâ, the year 113, *i. e.*, 421 A. D., that at Mandasor, the year 493 of the Mâlava era, corresponding to 437 A. D., and that at Mankuwar the year 129 *i. e.*, 447 A. D. The latest known date of Chandragupta II. is 411 A D. and the earliest of Kumâragupta 414, wherefore the latter must have acceded to the throne in the interval between those two years. Kumâragupta was followed by his son Skandagupta, of whom we have five inscriptions. One of them, that at Junâgaḍh in Kâṭhiawâḍ, represents the dyke of the celebrated Sudarśana lake to have burst in 136 and to have been repaired in 137. These years correspond to 454 and 455 A. D. Another at Kahâuṁ, Gorakhpur district, North-Western Provinces bears the year 141, corresponding to 459 A. D.; a third, engraved on a copperplate, and found in a stream at Indor in the Bulandshahr District, gives the year 146, *i. e.*, 464 A D. There is another at Bihâr, and the last or fifth is engraved on a pillar at Bhitâri, Ghazipur district, North-Western Provinces.[54] In this inscription a new foreign race makes its appearance for

---

54 *Ib.*. Nos. 12-16.

the first time—that of the Hûnas or Huns. Skandagupta is represented to have defeated them and to have subjugated a tribe of the name of Pushyamitras. After Skandagupta, the power of the dynasty began to decline. A Bhitarî seal inscription reveals the names of three of his successors, viz., his brother Puragupta, his son Narasiṁhagupta, and his son Kumâragupta (II). Perhaps for this last prince has been furnished the date G. E. 154 (c. A. D. 474) by a Sârnâth epigraph. A later date, viz., 157 is supplied by two Sârnâth inscriptions for apparently his successor Buddhagupta. There is an inscription at Eraṇ in the Sâgar district which also bears the name of Buddhagupta, and the date 165, corresponding to 483 A. D.

HUNAS OR HUNS AND THE AULIKARAS.

In the inscription of the reign of Buddhagupta mentioned above a Brahman Mahârâja of the name of Mâtṛi-Vishṇu and his brother Dhanya-Vishnu record the erection of a *Dhvajastambha* or flagstaff to the god Janârdana. In another of the first year of a prince named Toramâṇa, Dhanya-Vishṇu speaks of his brother Mâtṛi-Vishṇu as having died in the interval, and of his erecting a temple to the Boar or Varâha incarnation of Vishṇu.[56] There is another inscription at Gwalior, dated in the 15th year of Mihirakula, who is represented as Toramâṇa's son, and it records the erection of a temple of the sun by Mâtṛicheṭa.[57] Toramâṇa belonged to the Hûṇa race, so that it would appear that a short time after 174, G. E. or 492 A. D. the latest date of Buddhagupta occurring on one of his coins, *i. e.*, about 500 A. D., the Hûnas established their power up to the Central

---

Ib. No. 19.

Inscr. E. G. Kings, No. 36. *Ib.* No. 37.

Provinces. But since only two princes of the race are mentioned, it appears that they did not retain it for a long time. An inscription at Mandasor in Western Mâlwâ represents Yaśodharman to have subjugated Mihirakala. We have an inscription of the same prince, dated 589 of the Mâlava era corresponding to 533 A. D. The engraver of both is the same person, and his name was Govinda. From the manner in which the different statements are made in this inscription, it appears that the family of the prince, which was known by the epithet of Aulikara, was brought into importance by Vishṇuvardhana, who was a predecessor of Yaśodharman, and it was he who first assumed the title of " Supreme Lord, King of Kings." From this date of Yaśodharman, therefore, it may be safely concluded that the two Hûṇa princes could not have reigned for more than forty years on the Cis-Satlaj side of India.

VIGOROUS BRAHMANIC REVIVAL AND RENOVATION.—SUPERSESSION OF THE PRÂKṚITS BY THE SANSKRIT.

Now, in Chandragupta s inscription at Mathurâ, and Skandagupta's Bihar and Bhihâri inscriptions, Samudragupta is represented as having performed the Aśvamedha, which is pointedly spoken of as having gone out of use for a long time. This is the first instance of the Brahmanic revival under this dynasty. This achievement was considered so important that Samudragupta struck golden coins or medals, on the obverse of which is the figure of a horse let loose, and the title *Aśvamedha-parâkrama*, or " one who performed the achievement of a horse-sacrifice" on the reverse. Similar coins bearing on the reverse the legend *Aśvamedha-Mahendra*

58 *Ib*. No. 33. 59 *Ib*. No. 35.

60 Jour. R. A. S., Jan. 1889. p. 65.

have been found. *Mahendra* was a title assumed by Kumâragupta, as is evident from some of his coins on which his proper name as well as the title occur. It appears, therefore, that he too performed the horse-sacrifice indicative of supreme sovereignty. Chandragupta II., Kumâragupta, and Skandagupta are called Parama-Bhâgavatas on their coins, which shows that they were worshippers of Bhagavad Vâsudeva. One of the two Udayagiri inscriptions dated 82 G.E. = 400 A. D. is engraved on a panel over two figures,—one of a four-armed god attended by two female figures, and the other of a twelve-armed goddess. The god may be Vishṇu and the goddess Chaṇḍî. The other Udayagiri inscription records the dedication of a cave to Sambhu. The Bilsâḍ inscription of Kumâragupta speaks of the building of a Pratolî or gallery in the temple of Swâmi-Mahâsena by Dhruvasarman in the year 414 A. D. The Bihâr inscription represents the erection of a *yûpa* or a sacrificial post, and that on the Bhitâri pillar records the installation of an image of Śârṅgin and the grant of a village by Skandagupta. In the Junâgaḍh inscription, a temple of Chakrabhrit (Vishnu) is spoken of as having been erected in 456 A. D. by Chakrapâlita, son of Parṇadatta, Skandagupta's governor of Surâshṭra. The Indore inscription of the time of Skandagupta records the endowment of Devavishṇu in 464 A. D. for lighting a lamp in a temple of the sun. The Mandasor inscription speaks of the erection of a temple of the sun by a guild of weavers in 437 A. D. and its repair by the same in 473 A. D. According to Buddhagupta's Eraṇ inscription, Mâtrivishṇu and his brother Dhanyavishṇu erected, as mentioned above, a *Dhvajastambha*, or flagstaff, to the god Janârdana in 483 A.D. Mâtrivishṇu is

61 *Ib.* pp. 110, 105, 103.

called "a great devotee of Bhagavat," *i.e.*, Vishṇu. The inscriptions of minor chiefs and private individuals during this period record grants of villages to Brahmans, in the years 474, 481, 492, 495, and 509 A. D., to the temples of Pishṭapurî (527 A. D. and 532 A. D.) Bhagavat or Vishṇu (495 A. D.), and Âditya or the sun, (511 A. D.), the erection of a *dhvaja* of Vishṇu, grants of villages for the performance of the five great rites, (570 A. D.), the erection of a yûpa, or sacrificial post on the completion of a Puṇḍarîka sacrifice, the establishment of Sattras or feeding places for Brahmans and others &c., &c.

Here we have ample evidence of a powerful upheaval; and the sacrificial rites and the gods and goddesses adopted into the Brahmanic Pantheon to which, except in one instance, there was not even an allusion in the epigraphical records of the country for more than five centuries, suddenly present themselves to our view about the end of the fourth century; and appear uninterruptedly for the whole of the subsequent period of about two centuries covered by the inscriptions published in a collected form by Dr. Fleet. The worship of Siva, Vishṇu, the Sun and Mahâsena seems to have become popular with all classes from princes and chiefs to ordinary individuals. But a still more significant change is the universal adoption of the Sanskrit language for the documents inscribed on stone and metal

62 अत्यन्तभगवद्भक्त.

63 Inscr. E. G. Nos. 21, 22, 26, 27, 28

64 *Ib.* Nos. 25 and 31.

65 *Ib.* No. 27.

66 *Ib.* No. 28.

67 *Ib.* No. 32.

68 *Ib.* No. 38.

69 *Ib.* No. 59. The date of the Inscription is 428; but the Era is not specified. If it is the Mâlava Era the date is 372 A. D.; if the Saka, is 506 A. D. I incline to the latter supposition.

70 *Ib.* No. 64.

instead of the Pâli or Prâkṛit. It indicates the enhancement of Brahmanic influence. The Vernacular dialects had acquired such an importance that not only were they mostly used, as we have seen, in inscriptions, but a number of literary works presupposed by Hâla's Saptaśatî and others like the Bṛihatkathâ attributed to Gunâḍhya were composed in them in the second or third century of the Christian era. Buddhism had, of course, used one of them for all its religious and literary purposes. But now we find that Sanskrit, or the language of learned Brahmans, rose in general estimation and cquired such an over whelming importance that the Vernaculars were driven out of the field. It was more generally studied, and a new and more brilliant period in the history of Sanskrit literature dawned about this time.

REVIVAL IN THE SOUTH.

The influence of this vigorous Brahmanical revival in the north extended itself to the Dekkan. Of the early Châlukyas whose dynasty was established about the end of the fifth century, Pulakeśî I. solemnised the Asvamedha sacrifice and several other princes belonging to the family performed the other great sacrifices, and grants of land were made to Brahmans. A cave temple to Vishṇu was dedicated by Maṅgalîsa in Śaka 500 or 578 A. D., at Bâdâmî. And other temples to the same god and Siva or Maheśvara were constructed in several other places. The worship of Śiva in the terrific form of Kâpâlikeśvara seems also to have come into existence.

DECLINE OF BUDDHISM—RISE OF MAHÂYÂNISM.

While Brahmanism thus rose in importance and popular favour, the influence of Buddhism declined in a corresponding degree. The number of records of

Buddhist gifts during this period is smaller. In the Sâñchi inscription of Chandragupta (411 A. D.) is recorded a grant by a royal military officer for feeding ten Buddhist mendicants and lighting two lamps in the jewel-house.[71] The Mânkuwar inscription of Kumâragupta (447 A. D.) records the installation of an image of Buddha by a Bhikshu of the name of Buddhamitra.[72] Harisvâmini, wife of Sanasiddha, records in 449 A. D. in an inscription at Sâñchi the grant of twelve Dînâras as a fixed capital out of the interest on which a mendicant belonging to the Âryasaṁgha was to be fed daily, and of three Dînâras for the jewel-house out of the interest on which three lamps were to be daily lighted before the Blessed Buddha, and of one Dînâra for the seats of four Buddhas out of the interest on which a lamp was to be lighted daily at the seats. An image of Buddha was set up at Mathura in 453 A. D., another in 548 A. D., and others at Deoriyâ in the Allahabad District, Kasiâ in the Gorakpur District and in Buddhagayâ. The last was set up by Mahânâman who also constructed a temple (Prâsâda) of Lokaśâstṛe in 587 A. D. The language of these inscriptions unlike that of those of the preceding period is Sanskrit and it will be seen that images of Buddha were set up and worshipped like those of the Brahmanic gods. In both these respects it cannot be denied that Buddhism became subject to the same influences which were in operation in the case of Brahmanism, or rather appropriated those points in the rival system which increased its popularity about this time. The principles of faith in personal beings and devotion to them were incorporated into their creed ; and Sanskrit was resorted to confer dignity on their religious books

---

71 *Ib.* No. 5. 72 *Ib.* No. 11.
73 *Ib.* No. 62. 74 *Ib.* Nos. 63, 70, 68, 69 and 72. 75 *Ib.* Nos 71.

and teachers. The use of this learned language shows at the same time, that, like Brahmanism, Buddhism now assumed a more exclusive character and ceased to appeal to the people at large in their own language; and the sphere of its influence became much narrow. Thus it appears that the revival and renovation of Brahmanism went on side by side with corresponding changes in Buddhism which impressed on it the form and character known by the name of Mahâyâna. The earlier form of Buddhism appealing only to the moral feelings of man had split up into a number of schools and exhausted itself; and its place was taken up by Brahmanism and Mahâyânism. But the charm of the names Buddha Dharma, and Saṁgha, the three jewels, was lost; and Mahâyânism was unable to regain what had been lost by primitive Buddhism. Compared with revived Brahmanism it was feeble; and from the first it had to face the severe attacks of its renovated rival.

THE JAINAS.

We have two Jaina inscriptions also in this period recording the installation of images in the years 424 A.D and 459 A. D., at Udayagiri and Kahâuṁ respectively. Another inscription of the reign of Kumâragupta dated 113 G. E. or 431 A. D. records the setting up of an image at Mathurâ.[77] It would thus appear that tha religion had not many adherents or patrons about this time.

CAUSES OF THE PREVIOUS DECLINE OF BRAHMANISM AND ITS REVIVAL AND RENOVATION AT THIS PERIOD.

The vigorous Brahmanical revival we have been considering must have been due, in a large measure, to

76 *Ib.* Nos. 61 and 15.

77 Ep. Ind., vol. II., p. 210.

the natural decay of early Buddhism. It was this Buddhism that had supplanted Brahmanism in popular favour, and for the four or five centuries that it enjoyed the ascendancy it had acquired, Brahmanism and the sanskrit language and literature were neglected. The Brahmans themselves regarded their decline as due to the triumph of Buddhism. Subandhu in one of his puns in the Vâsavadattâ tells us that the Bauddha doctrine had brought about the destruction of the system based on the words of the Veda. If so, the Brahmanic revival must be regarded as synchronous with the decline of early Buddhism and the rise of Mahâyânism. According to all accounts it was Nâgârjuna, the contemporary of Kanishka, that gave a distinct form to this Buddhism though the movement may have begun a little earlier. As according to our view, Kanishka reigned in the last quarter of the third century, the revival of Brahmanism must have already begun before that period. But the ascendancy of early Buddhism was not the only cause that had kept down Brahmanism. For about a century before Christ and three centuries and a half after, there was no powerful Brahmanic prince; and this is shown by the Gupta inscriptions already noticed, which state that the horse-sacrifice indicative of supreme sovereignty, had gone out of use for a long time, and also by the fact that no inscription or coin reports the existence of such a prince during the period. This circumstance must have been the result of the political condition of the country. It was overrun again and again by foreign invaders, each of whom established his power for a short time and had to yield to another. The Sakas of Mâlwâ and Kâṭhiâwâḍ only retained their sovereignty for about three hundred

---

78 कश्चिद्बौद्धसिद्धान्त इव क्षपितश्रुतिवचनदर्शनोभवत् । p. 297 Hall's Ed.

79 Wassiljew, Germ. Trans, p. 128.

years. The argument which has been advanced that these foreign princes held a comparatively small portion of the country, and could not have influenced its literary and religious condition for the worse has no weight. The unsettled condition of the country consequent on their frequent invasions rendered the rise of a supreme Brahmanic ruler impossible; and the foreigners themselves could not be expected to favour Brahmanism in a manner to enable it to deprive Buddhism of its ascendancy. Some of them were no doubt Hinduized, but they were not Brahmanized. And the Brahmans themselves complained of their being neglected by the Yavanas, Śakas and Pahlavas, as will hereafter be shown in connection with a passage from Manu and the Mahâbhârata.

PATRONS OF THE BRAHMANIC REVIVAL AND RENOVATION—WEMA-KADPHISES.

Wema-Kadphises however seems to have become a more thorough Hindu than any other foreign prince, and in his time the Brahmanic revival may be understood to have truly begun. *i.e.*, in the middle of the third century of the Christian era. We have seen that his coins bear a figure of Nandin and Śiva on the reverse, and he styles himself a worshipper of Maheśvara or a member of the Maheśvara sect. The Śakas had figures of Greek deities on their coins, and there are no distinct indications on them, or on those of the Parthians, of any Indian deity But with Wema-Khadphises what might almost be called a revolution in this respect begins. His Kushâna successors continue their respect for Brahmanic deities, but extend it also to those of the Greeks and Zoroastrians, as well as to Buddha. Kadphises, however, could not have been a patron of the old Vedic religion, nor of Brahmans in particular as a sacred caste, nor of the

Sanskrit language and literature. An all-sided revival and renovation could proceed only under the patronage of Hindu princes. And such were the Guptas.

THE GUPTAS—SAMUDRAGUPTA AND CHANDRA GUPTA II. OR VIKRAMÂDITYA ŚAKÂRI.

The fact that the inscriptions recording gifts to Brahmanic deities and for the daily sacrifices begin about the end of the fourth century shows unmistakeably that the Brahmanic revival derived its force and vigor from the patronage of the Gupta princes. Samudragupta and Kumâragupta performed, as we have seen, the horse-sacrifice, which had gone out of use. The former is represented in his Allahabad inscription to have acquired the title of "Prince of poets" by writing works which served as models for learned men or pleased them. He patronized poets, and thus put an end to the hostility between good poetry and worldly prosperity. The tradition about a Vikramâditya, who was *Sakâri* or enemy of the Śakas and drove them and other foreigners out of the country and patronized learning, is appropriately applicable only to Chandragupta II. of all the princes who flourished before him and after, and whose names have come down to us. For he conquered Mâlwâ, as we have seen, before 400 A. D., and probably in 388 or 389 A. D. and exterminated the Śakas, *i.e.*, the Satraps of Mâlwâ, whose latest date is 388 A. D., and drove out the Kushanas since he is the earliest Gupta prince whose inscription is found at Mathurâ, a town which belonged to the Kushanas. He assumed the title of Vikramâditya, which we find on his coins. He made Ujjayinî his

80 विद्वज्जनोपजीव्यानेककाव्यक्रियाभिः प्रतिष्ठितकविराजशब्दस्य. L. 27.

81 सत्काव्यश्रीविरोधान्बुधगुणितगुणाज्ञाहतानेव कृत्वा

82 See D. R. Bhandarkar's paper, pp. (31-23).

83 Jour. R. A. S., Jan. 1889, pp. 91, 82, 78, 76.

capital. For, certain chieftains of the name of Guttas (Guptas) of Guttal in the Dhârwâr district give themselves in their inscriptions the title of *Ujjayanîpuravarâdhîśvara*, which, like similar titles, found in other places signifies that they belonged to a family which once reigned in glory at Ujjayinî. They trace their descent through Víkramâditya, specified as king of Ujjayinî, and are styled full moons of the ocean of nectar in the shape of the lineage of Chandragupta. Ujjayinî was thus the capital of the Guptas from whom the Dharwar Guptas derived their descent. The Chandragupta and Vikramâditya mentioned in their inscriptions are, it will be observed, one and the same person, and it is but right that he should be mentioned above all ; for it was he who drove away the foreigners and first established himself at Ujjayinî. In one place, however, instead of *Ujjayinî* we have *Pâṭalî* in the title, showing that Pâṭaliputra the original capital, had not been forgotten by the Southern Guptas. There is no other Vikramâditya whose existence is authenticated by any contemporary document and who can be construed as the destroyer of Śakas. The supposition of the existence of one in the middle of the sixth century has no ground to stand on. Now though Chandragupta II. was Vikramâditya Sakâri, the patron of learning, it is by no means necessary to suppose that all the celebrated nine gems flourished at his court. Tradition often jumbles together persons and things belonging to different times and places. Varâhamihira, who died in 509 Śaka, or 587 A. D., and the epoch year of whose *Pañchasiddhântikâ* is 427 Śaka, or 505 A. D., cannot have flourished at the court of Chandragupta-Vikramâditya who died between 411 and 414 A. D.

---

84 *Bombay Gazetteer*, Vol. I, Part II Dr. Fleet's Dynasties of the Kanarese District p. 578,

But that Vikramâditya Sakâri was a patron of learning is stated by the *Râjataranginî*. He is said to have made a poet of the name of Mâtṛigupta, king of Kaśmîr, and Mâtrigupta had a poet dependent on him of the name of Meṇṭha or Bhartṛimeṇṭha, so that these two were contemporaries of Chandragupta-Vikramâditya. The date assigned by Cunningham to Mâtṛigupta is 430 A. D. which is not far removed from that of the Gupta prince as determined from his inscriptions. Meṇṭha has been associated with Vikramâditya by the compilers of anthologies who ascribe a certain verse to their joint authorship.

KÂLIDÂSA.

And some of the nine gems, perhaps Kâlidâsa himself, may have lived during the reign of Chandragupta-Vikramâditya. Mallinâṭha in his comment on verse 14 of the Meghadûṭa, states that there is in that verse an implied allusion to an opponent of Kâlidâsa, named Diṅnâga. This person is supposed to be the same as the celebrated Buddhist logician of that name, known also to Brahmanic writers; and the supposition is, I think, very probable. He is said to have been a pupil of a Buddhist patriarch of the name of Vasubandhu ; and the date of the latter, and consequently that of his pupil and of Kâlidâsa, has been determined by Professor Max Müller to be the middle of the sixth century. But the Professor goes, I think, upon the chronological traditions reported by the Chinese, and does not attach due weight to certain facts which necessitate our placing Vasubandhu earlier. One of Vasubandhu's works was translated into Chinese in the year 404 A. D. and another about the year 405

---

85 लिम्पतीव तमोङ्गानि वर्षतीवाञ्जनं नभः which occurs in the *Mrichchhakatika*.

A. D. This shows that Vasubandhu must have flourished before 404 A. D. At the same time the Chinese authorities make him a contemporary of King Vikramâditya of Śrâvasti, or of Sâketa, since the town was situated in that province. If he was a contemporary of that King, the King may have lived in the last quarter of the fourth century. Sâketa, or Ayodhyâ, over which he ruled was a province belonging to the Guptas; and the attitude of the King towards the Bauddhas was hostile, as he convoked assemblies of learned Buddhists and Brahmans, for religious disputations, in which the former were defeated and lost the King's support. For these reasons the Vikramâditya, whose contemporary Vasubandhu was, must in all likelihood have been the Brahmanic Gupta prince Chandragupta-Vikramâditya. And if he held his court at Śrâvastî and is represented to have ruled over Sâketa, the time referred to must be that previous to the conquest of Mâlwâ, which took place about 389 A. D., and after which the King in all probability resided at Ujjayinî. Vasubandhu therefore lived in the last quarter of the fourth century; and his pupil Diṅnâga, about the end of that century; and if Kâlidâsa was his contemporary, he too must have lived about that time and thus have been one of the gems at Vikramâditya's court.

LITERARY REVIVAL AND RENOVATION.

If then after several centuries of neglect on the part of princes and people, Brahmanism began to rise in influence and importance under Wema-Kadphises about

---

86 Cat. Bunyiu Nanjio, Nos. 1188 and 1218.

87 Wassiljew, Germ. Trans., p. 84.

88 Hiuen Tsiang's Travels, Beal's Trans. Vol. I., p. 106 ff.; Wassiljew Germ, Trans., p 240.

the middle of the third century after Christ, and made rapid strides in the time of the Gupta Emperors, we might expect the Brahmans to make every effort to widen their influence and render it permanent. And this is what, I think, we do find. With that object they gave a new and more popular shape to the literature of their creed and rearranged it in a manner to meet the wants and be in harmony with the changed feelings of an increased number of followers, and strengthen their hold over them. They made a great endeavour to place it on a philosophical basis and show that the creed of their opponents had no such basis. This, therefore, was the age when metrical Smṛitis, Purâṇas, and Bhâshyas or commentaries containing explanatory, apologetic, and controversial matter began to be written; and the general literary impulse was communicated to other branches of learning including poetry. We shall now proceed to the elucidation of this point.

WORKS ON RELIGIOUS LAW.

In the olden times, the works on religious law existed in the form of Sûtras or prose aphorisms, and they were identified with particular schools or Śâkhâs of Brahmans. We have thus the Dharma and Gṛihya Sûtras of Âpastamba, of Baudhâyana, Kaṭha, Âśvalâyana, &c. But afterwards books written in Anushṭubh ślokas came to be used. They prescribed the same rules as those given in the Dharma and Gṛihya Sûtras, and in some cases a close resemblance has been found to exist between the words and expressions used in the Sûtras and the metrical Law-books or Smṛitis. Thus the Sûtras on the Vinâyakaśânti in the Kaṭha Sûtra are reproduced almost word for word in the corresponding portion of the Yâjñavalkya Smṛiti. But in the new books the

89 See Bradke on Mânava Gr. S. Jour. Germ. Or. S., vol. XXXVI., p. 427ff.

exposition is plainer than in the Sûtras, which were primarily meant to be supplemented by oral explanation. Here, therefore, is an attempt to disentangle the Brahmanic religious law from the narrow schools to which it was before attached, and put it in a form intelligible and applicable to all Brahmanic Hindus. Hence is the choice of the Anushṭubh śloka instead of the old Sûtras, as it was used ordinarily for all literary purposes. But in the revised Hindu Law certain customs such as the killing of cows even for sacrificial purposes, and levirate, the feeling against which had grown strong, were prohibited; while a compromise was effected in the case of others which had not become unpopular to that extent. The old precept, for instance, about eating the flesh of five species of animals was hedged round by a number of restrictions; but in order to satisfy the claims of the old Vedic religion, the slaughter of some of them was freely allowed in religious rites. These metrical Smṛitis therefore, it would not be wrong to refer to about the Kushana—Gupta period. There is a passage in the Smṛiti of Manu, in which it is stated that certain native Indian tribes, such as the Puṇḍrakas and the Draviḍas, and the Yavanas, Śakas, and Pahlavas, were originally Kshatriyas, but they became Sûdras by their setting the Brahmans at defiance and gradually ceasing to perform the religious rites.[90] In a chapter in the Ânuśâsanika Book of the Mahâbhârata, Bhîshma says to Yudhishṭhira "that the highest duty of a crowned king is to worship learned Brahmans; they should be protected as one protects oneself or one's children; and be respected, bowed to, and revered as if they were one's parents. If Brahmans are contented, the whole country prospers; if they are discontented and angry, everything goes to

90 X.43.44.

destruction. They can make a god not a god, and a not-god a god. One whom they praise prospers, one whom they reproach, becomes miserable. The different Kshatriya tribes, Śakas, Yavanas, and Kâmbojas became Śûdras through not seeing or following Brahmans."[91] In these passages a Kshatriya orgin is supposed in order that the Śûdrahood of these tribes, which was consequent on their being beyond the Âryan pale and which, as stated before, is plainly asserted by Patañjali in the case of two of them, may appear as the result of their not paying deference to Brahmans. This shows that the neglect of the sacerdotal caste by the Yavanas, Śakas, Pahlavas and other tribes was uppermost in the minds of those who invented a Kshatriya origin for them; and the passages and especially the chapter in the Mahâbhârata look as if they were written when the foreign domination had come to a close and the Brahmans had fully triumphed, and were anxious to preserve their newly gained influence. The chapter, therefore, must have been interpolated into the epic in the Gupta period, and the Smṛiti of Manu based on a previous Sûtra work and traditional or floating texts, composed at about the same time. The Mahâbhârata, however, already existed in its full form at the period; for it is mentioned by name in copperplate inscriptions of the years 174 G. E. (492-3 A.D.) and 177 G.E. (495-6 A. D.) and two more, and as a Śatasâbasrî or a work of a hundred thousand verses in one of the year 214 G. E. (532-3 A. D.)[93] But it can hardly admit of a reasonable doubt that it was retouched about this period.

---

91 Chap. 33. 92 See below, p. 49.

93 Dr. Fleet's Early Gupta Inscr. Nos. 26, 27, 28, 30 and 31.

WORKS ON THE SACRIFICIAL RITUAL.

The works on the sacrificial ritual and especially the Bhâshyas or great commentaries on the Sûtras of the several Vedas or Śâkhas must have begun to be written about this time. Since the sacrificial religion was being revived, the necessity of a definite and authoritative ritual was felt; and as the sacrifices had been out of use for a long time, knowledge of the ritual was rare and vague. The names of the writers of the Bhâshyas and other works on the ritual end in the honorific title of *Svâmin*, such as a Devasvâmin, the commentator on the Sûtra of Âśvalâyana; Bhavasvâmin, on that of Baudhâyana; Dhûrtasvâmin on that of Âpastamba; Agnisvâmin on that of Latyâyana, &c. This title we find used in Central India in the last quarter of the fifth century and the first of the sixth. In the copperplate charter dated 474-5 A. D. 481-2 A.D. and 509-10 A. D. issued by the Parivrâjaka Mahârâjas occur such names as Gopasvâmin, Bhavasvâmin, Devasvâmin the son of Agnisvâmin, Govindasvâmin, &c., among the grantees. In the Dekkan we find the title affixed to the names of some of the grantees in the copperplates issued by the princes of the early Châlukya dynasty in the second half of the seventh century and the early part of the eighth; and we have such names as Keśavasvâmin, Karkasvâmin, and Devasvâmin which are the names of writers of commentaries on the sacrificial Sûtras and other works on the ritual. The title *Svâmin* is indicative of the period between the fourth and the tenth centuries; for we do not find it used later.

PURÂṆAS.

The idea of recasting the Purâṇas into their present form must have originated about this time. They existed

94 Fleet E. G. Inscr. No. 21. 95 Ib. No. 22. 96 Ib. No. 23.

long before, since they are alluded to in the Upanishads and Śrautasûtras, but their contents must have been strictly in accordance with the rule given by Amarasiṁha in his lexicon, and embraced an account of the creation and dissolution of the world, of the different families of Ṛishis and princes, and the deeds of the most heroic among them, and of the Manvantaras or different ages of the world. But now the necessity of glorifying the different gods and goddesses whose worship was rising in favour and of firmly inculcating other religious duties had been felt; and new Purâṇas were composed having the framework of the old but with new matter introduced on every occasion. Thus, if we compare the chapters on Creation in the Vâyu, the Liṅga, and Mârkaṇḍeya Purâṇas, we shall find not only a similarity of contents but of language also. The Vishṇu contains an abridged account of the matter but oftentimes the words are the same. Most of the existing Puraṇas, perhaps all, were written to promote the worship of particular deities. Vishṇu, Śiva, and Durgâ in their several forms, or to strengthen the authority of the religious practices that had begun to prevail. The Vâyu appears to be one of the oldest of these works, as it is quoted in Śaṁkarâchârya's Bhâshya. It mentions the Guptas, as I have already observed, as ruling alongside of the Gaṅgâ, over Prayâga, Sâketa and Magadha. If this verse has undergone no corruption and was advisedly put in the Purâṇa in which we find it must have been written before Chandragupta-Vikramâditya conquered Mâlwâ and Mathurâ and drove out the foreigners, that is, before the last quarter of the fourth century. The Vishṇu has the text in a corrupt form. As the Purâṇa editors did not care very much for the matter which did not immediately concern their purpose, they were not careful to give the original before them correctly and even misunderstood it. The Vishṇu is evidently later than the Vâyu. The Purâṇas began to be recast when the worship of Hindu deities rose in popular estimation about the time of Wema-Kadphises *circa* 250 A. D., and the process continued ihrough the Gupta period to a much later date and new Purâṇas appeared from time to time; and it has hardly ceased even to this day, since we find Mâhâtmyas springing up now and then though not Purâṇas in a complete shape.

FLOATING LITERATURE.

In considering the question of the recasting of the works on the religious creed of the Brahmans and those on mythology, it should be borne in mind that the art of writing was introduced into India at a comparatively late period, and even afterwards was resorted to very rarely. Hence literary works and detached verses containing religious and moral precepts and beautiful poetic sentiments were, in the olden times, composed and transmitted orally. In the case of the latter the name of the author was forgotten; and there was thus a floating mass of anonymous verses in the mouths of the learned. When therefore systematic writing had to be resorted to, to give fixity and permanence to the creed, and when it came to be generally used even for purposes of profane literature, these floating verses were appropriated or used by several writers. Hence it is that we often find the same verses in such works as the Smṛiti of Manu, the Mahâbhârata, and even in Pâli Buddhistic works, and sometimes, though very rarely, in dramatic plays and poems also. This source, therefore, was also drawn upon by the writers of Smṛitis and Purâṇas in the Gupta period, in addititon to those already indicated.

ASTRONOMY

Like the Dharma and the legendary-lore, the astronomy of the Hindus was also recast on the same principle as that which guided the re-edition of those two branches, *viz.*, to put it in a form suited to the condition of the new times. Hence the old astronomical elements were combined with such ones of a Greek origin as had found acceptance among the Hindus and some new elements discovered or thought out by the writers themselves being added, the works known as the original five Siddhântas arose.[97] As in the case of the new works on the first two subjects, the name of a profane author was not connected with these works; but it was expressly stated or left to be understood that they were composed by old Munis or gods. Dr. Thibaut thinks that two of them the Romaka and the Paulîsa must have been composed not later than 400 A. D. Probably all the Siddhântas were written about the middle of the fourth century or even earlier, especially as they were held in reverence by Varâhamihira who wrote about them in the middle of the sixth century. A direct borrowing from any particular Greek work is not contended for by any body. As in the case of the art of coinage, the knowledge of some elements of Greek astronomy must have reached the Hindus through the Bactrians, the Śakas, and the other foreign races with whom they came in contact; and this was made use of in their works when the Brahmans gained or regained influence in the fourth century. All the celebrated Indian astronomers flourished after this period. Âryabhata was born in 476 A. D. and Varâhamihira died, as already stated, in 587 A. D.

97 See Dr. Thibaut's Intr. to his Ed. of the Pañchasiddhântikâ pp. xlix to l.

MIMÂṀSÂ.

Subandhu in his Vâsavadattâ tells us that the doctrine of Tathâgata or Buddha was destroyed or attacked by those who followed the system of Jaimini.[98] The earliest of these followers whose works are extant is Śabarasvâmin, the author of the Mîmâṁsâbhâshya Śabarasvâmin establishes the existence of the soul as an independent entity and not identical with the feelings, which are phenomenal only, against the Bauddhas generally, and the reality of the external world against the followers of the Yogâchâra School, and refutes the nihilism taught by the Mâdhyamika School.[99] The Yogâchâra School was founded by Âryâsaṅga, or Asaṅga, who was the elder brother of Vasubandhu, the preceptor of Diṅnâgâchârya. Âryâsaṅga was thus a contemporary of Vasubandhu,[100] and lived in the last quarter of the fourth century. Śabarasvâmin, therefore, probably composed his Bhâshya, on Jaimini, in the fifth century and we have seen that the honorific title, *Svâmin* which he bore, was in use in that century. Kumârila was the writer of a Vârtika on the Bhâshya, and he was a strong combatant. He flourished about the end of the seventh century. There was another school of the Mîmâṁsâ, thoroughly atheistic, founded by Prabhâkara. But it appears to have been soon neglected. All these writers laboured also to establish the authoritativeness of the Vedas and their eternity against the objections urged by the Buddhists and Jainas.

---

98 In the run contained in the expression केचिज्जैमिनिमतानुसारिण इव तथा गतमतध्वंसिनः ।

99 Ed. Bibl. Ind. pp. 19ff.. 8, 9. Kumarilâ, in his Slokavârtika indicates that Sabara refutes in the last two cases the doctrines of the Yogâchâra and Mâdhyamika Schools.

100 Was siljew, Germ. Trans, pp. 146, 226 and 237.

LOGIC, DIALECTICS, AND SÂṀKHYA.

Buddhists and Brahmans carried on controversies in the field of logic also. The well-known passage in the beginning of Vâchaspati's work, entitled Vârtikatâtparyaṭîkâ, gives us valuable imformation about the matter. "The revered Akshapâda having composed the Śâstra calculated to lead to eternal bliss, and an exposition of it having been given by Pakshilasvâmin, what is it that remains and requires that a Vartika should be composed? Though the author of the Bhâshya has given an exposition of the Śâstra, still modern (scholars) Diṅnaga and others having enveloped it in the darkness of fallacious arguments, that exposition is not sufficient for determining the truth; hence the author of the Uddyota dispels the darkness by his work the Uddyota, *i.e.*, light (torch)."[101] Vâchaspati here calls Diṅnâga a modern in comparison with Pakshilasvâmin or Vâtsyâyana, the author of the Bhâshya. If he had correct information, Vâtsyâyana must be supposed to have lived about two or more centuries before Diṅnâga. But it can hardly be expected that he should have a correct historical knowledge of the matter. It is, therefore, not unlikely, especially in view of the fact that the title *Svâmin* is given to the author, that he flourished about half a century before Diṅnâga, *i. e.*, about the middle of the fourth century. Bhâradvâja or the author of the Uddyota, is, as is well known, mentioned by Subandhu, who again is praised by Bâṇa in the middle of the seventh century. He may therefore have flourished in the middle of the sixth century, or even earlier. In later times Buddhist doctrines in logic and metaphysics were critised by the Vedântins Śaṁkarâchârya and his pupil Sureśvara. The

101 Sec. Ed. in the Vizianagram Series, p. 1.

102 2nd Ed. Sâmkhyasâra, Preface, p. 29. I understand the passage ईश्वरकृष्णनाम्ना कालिदासेन कृताः कारिकाः as in the text.

Śâṁkhya[1] philosophy also was revived by Îśvarakṛishṇa who wrote the Sâṁkhya Kârikâs. The oldest commentary, on the work is that by Gauḍapâdâchârya. The Kârikâs and the commentary were translated into Chinese between the years 557 A. D. and 569 A. D. The Kârikâs are in the Âryâ metre, and this metre is used by Âryabhata and others, and appears to have been a favourite with the writers of the period. An author quoted by Dr. Hall says that Kâlidâsa composed the Kârikâs in the name of Îśvarakṛishṇa, or using the name Îśvarakṛishṇa. Whether this is true or not all that we know about the Îśvarakṛishṇa is not inconsistent with the supposition that he flourished in the beginning of the fifth century.

ORNATE POETRY.

Sanskrit poetry was cultivated and appreciated more generally in this period than it could have been in the preceding ages, when the language itself was not generally studied and the Prâkṛits were in favour. I have already spoken about Kâlidâsa and Bhartṛimeṇṭha. Though the dates of all the poets from whose works we have excerpts in our anthologies are not known, my general feeling is that none of the writers of ornate poetry quoted therein is older than the fourth or the end of the third century. Aśvaghosha, the author of the Buddhacharita, which has often been compared to Kâlidâsa's Raghuvaṁśa, was a contemporary of Kanishka, as is admitted by all, and lived, according to our interpretation of the Kushâna dates, at the end of the third and the beginning of the fourth century. Professor Max Müller started several years ago the theory of the "Renaissance of Sanskrit Literature." It was powerfully contested by several able scholars, and now it seems almost to have been given up. But there is no question that the inscriptions place clearly before us the facts of the decline of Brahmanism, the ascendancy of early Buddhism, and the neglect of the Sanskrit language and cultivation of the Prâkṛits, from about the first century before Christ to about the middle of the fourth, and a powerful Brahmanic revival about the end of the century. This phenomenon may be called "Revival and Renovation of Brahmanism and of the Sanskrit Language and Literature." Professor Max Müller placed the Śakâri Vikramâditya in the middle of the sixth century, and assigned that period to the nine gems and later dates to the whole of modern Sanskrit literature. I have identified him with Chandragupta-Vikramâditya of the Gupta dynasty, who reigned about the end of the fourth century, and referred Kâlidâsa to that period. Under this supposition most of the arguments used by the late Professor Bühler lose their weight; and the only Sanskrit inscription left for him to go upon is that of Rudradâman at Girnar of the year 150 A. D. But according to my way of understanding the matter, ornate poetry was not undeveloped or unknown in the centuries of Brahmanic depression; but the language chiefly used for its cultivation was one or other of the Prâkṛits or Vernaculars, and Sanskrit was resorted to rarely. I attach full weight to the argument based upon the specimens of Sanskrit poetry occurring in the Mahâbhâshya. But I maintain that, like Brahmanism itself, it had not many votaries and was not extensively cultivated. With the restoration of Brahmanic influence in the Gupta period, it received a fresh start along with the other branches of literature we have passed under review; and just as there were earlier works in those branches, so were these earlier poetic works. The decline in the previous period was due not to any positive hostility of the foreign rulers, but to the popularity of early Buddhism and of the Prâkṛit languages ; and the only way in which the foreigners exercised a baneful influence was, as has been already indicated, by not patronizing Brahmanic learning in the manner in which a Brahmanic universal sovereign would have done, and rendering, by their frequent incursions and their power, the rise of such a one impossible.